CW01187852

Books in the series "Crafting your career in academia":

- Writing effective promotion applications (August 2022)
- Publishing in academic journals (November 2022)
- Creating social media profiles (February 2023)
- Measuring and improving research impact (May 2023)
- Using the Publish or Perish software (August 2023)

Publishing in academic journals

Crafting your career in academia

Anne-Wil Harzing

Edition: November 2022

ISBN 978-1-7396097-2-6 (paperback, black & white)

© 2010-2022 by Anne-Wil Harzing

All rights reserved. No part of this book may be reproduced in any form or by any electronic or mechanical means (including electronic mail, photocopying, recording, or information storage and retrieval) without permission in writing from the publisher.

As the SOLE exception to the above if you purchased this book in its PDF edition, then you are allowed to print 1 (one) hard copy for your own use only for each licence that you purchased.

Published by Tarma Software Research Ltd, UK

Author	Harzing, Anne-Wil
Title	Publishing in academic journals. Crafting your career in academia / Anne-Wil Harzing
Edition	1st ed.
ISBN	978-1-7396097-2-6 (paperback, black & white)
Subjects	Academic careers, academic publishing, academic development
Dewey Number	650.14

Table of contents

INTRODUCTION	**1**
CHAPTER 1: THE FOUR PS OF PUBLISHING	**3**
PERFORM: SUBMIT THE BEST PAPER YOU CAN	3
PRACTICE AND SEE FEEDBACK AS A GIFT	4
PARTICIPATE IN ACADEMIC NETWORKS	5
BUT MOST OF ALL: PERSIST, PERSIST, PERSIST	6
CHAPTER 2: HOW TO KEEP UP TO DATE WITH THE LITERATURE?	**9**
A SHORT HISTORY TOUR	9
DROWNING IN INFORMATION?	10
HOW TO KEEP YOUR HEAD ABOVE THE WATER?	11
1. SET UP CITATION ALERTS FOR YOUR OWN ARTICLES	11
2. SET UP NEW ARTICLE ALERTS FOR OTHER ACADEMICS	12
3. SET UP NEW ARTICLE ALERTS FOR KEY TOPICS IN YOUR FIELD	12
4. CHECK GOOGLE SCHOLAR'S "MY UPDATES" REGULARLY	12
5. SUBSCRIBE TO TABLE OF CONTENTS ALERTS	13
6. PERIODICALLY REVIEW CORE JOURNALS IN YOUR FIELD	13
IN SUM	13
CHAPTER 3: USING PUBLISH OR PERISH TO DO A LITERATURE REVIEW	**15**
COMPREHENSIVE LITERATURE REVIEW: BORN GLOBAL FIRMS	15
FOUNDING AUTHORS	16
HISTORICAL DEVELOPMENT OF THE FIELD	17
IMPORTANT JOURNALS	18
FOLLOW UP ON KEY PUBLICATIONS IN THE FIELD	19
IN SUM	20
HOW TO CONDUCT A LONGITUDINAL LITERATURE REVIEW?	**20**
WORKED EXAMPLE 1: CULTURE IN THE FIELD OF INTERNATIONAL BUSINESS	21
WORKED EXAMPLE 2: HIV IN SCIENCE, NATURE, AND CELL	22

CHAPTER 4: WHERE TO SUBMIT YOUR PAPER? 25

USE PUBLISH OR PERISH TO SEARCH FOR KEYWORDS	25
SORT THE RESULTS BY PUBLICATION OUTLET	26
WORKED EXAMPLE: ETHICAL MARKETING	**26**
JOURNAL OF BUSINESS ETHICS	27
JOURNAL OF MACROMARKETING	27
EUROPEAN JOURNAL OF MARKETING	28
JOURNAL OF CONSUMER MARKETING	30
JOURNAL OF PUBLIC POLICY & MARKETING	30
JOURNAL OF MARKETING EDUCATION	31
JOURNAL OF THE ACADEMY OF MARKETING SCIENCE	31
USING THE "TITLE WORDS" BOX TO FURTHER REFINE RESULTS	32
REVIEW KEY ACADEMICS IN YOUR FIELD	**33**
BEFORE SUBMISSION: HAVE YOU MISSED ANY PAPERS?	**35**
WORKED EXAMPLE: ENTRY MODES OF JAPANESE MNCS	35
NO PAPERS AT ALL?	37
CONCLUSION	**38**

CHAPTER 5: WHO DO YOU TALK TO? TARGETING JOURNALS 39

JOINING A CONVERSATION: CAUTION AND CARE	**39**
OR JUMPING RIGHT IN...	40
JOURNALS: COMMUNITIES & CONVERSATIONS	**40**
WHAT TO DO? RESEARCH, RESEARCH, RESEARCH	41
SUBMIT TO ONLY *ONE* JOURNAL AT A TIME	**43**
PUBLISHING YOUR WORK: ENGAGEMENT, DATING OR MARRIAGE?	44
HOW TO WRITE FOR US JOURNALS WITH NON-US DATA?	**45**
HOW TO AVOID PREDATORY JOURNALS?	**46**
MY RECOMMENDATIONS	47
PREDATORY JOURNALS: MORE THAN A FRINGE PHENOMENON	47
PREDATORY JOURNALS IN BUSINESS & MANAGEMENT	48
WANT TO KNOW MORE?	49
CONCLUSION	**50**

CHAPTER 6: HOW TO AVOID A DESK-REJECT? 51

WHY ARE DESK-REJECTS INCREASING?	**51**
ARE YOU READY? TEN PRACTICAL SIGNS	**53**
CONCLUSION	**55**

CHAPTER 7: YOUR TITLE: THE PUBLIC FACE OF YOUR PAPER — 57

A GOOD TITLE IS DESCRIPTIVE… — 57
… OR QUIRKY? TRY BOTH! — 58
HOW TO IMPROVE YOUR TITLE? — 59
SOME QUICK FINE-TUNING TIPS — 60

CHAPTER 8: WRITING YOUR ABSTRACT: NOT A LAST-MINUTE ACTIVITY — 63

WHAT NEEDS TO BE INCLUDED IN AN ABSTRACT? — 63
TWO EXAMPLE ABSTRACTS — 64
INTRODUCING A NEW CONCEPT TO THE FIELD — 65
PROVIDING EMPIRICAL RIGOUR TO EXISTING CONCEPTS — 65
SOME QUICK FINE-TUNING TIPS — 66

CHAPTER 9: YOUR INTRODUCTION: FIRST IMPRESSIONS COUNT! — 69

EMAILS VS. PAPER INTRODUCTIONS — 69
PROVIDE THE CONTEXT — 70
ARGUE FOR YOUR TOPIC'S IMPORTANCE — 70
WHAT'S IN IT FOR THE READER? — 73
HOW TITLE, ABSTRACT AND INTRODUCTION WORK IN HARMONY — 75
TITLE — 76
ABSTRACT — 76
INTRODUCTION — 77

CHAPTER 10: CONCLUSIONS: LAST IMPRESSIONS COUNT TOO! — 79

WHAT *DO* YOU INCLUDE IN CONCLUSIONS? — 79
THEORY/CONCEPT FOCUSED CONCLUSION — 80
CONTEXT/ACTION FOCUSED CONCLUSION — 81
HOW TO END YOUR PAPER EFFECTIVELY? — 82

CHAPTER 11: WHAT DO YOU CITE? USING REFERENCES STRATEGICALLY — 85

HOW TO USE REFERENCES STRATEGICALLY? — 86
SETTING THE SCENE — 86
REFERENCE THE EDITOR AND/OR REVIEWERS — 87
REFERENCE CORE THEORETICAL AND METHODOLOGICAL PUBLICATIONS — 88
TWELVE GUIDELINES FOR ACADEMIC REFERENCING — 88
1. REPRODUCE THE CORRECT REFERENCE — 89
2. REFER TO THE CORRECT PUBLICATION — 89

3.	DO NOT USE "EMPTY" REFERENCES	89
4.	USE RELIABLE SOURCES	90
5.	USE GENERALISABLE SOURCES FOR GENERALISED STATEMENTS	90
6.	DO NOT MISREPRESENT THE CONTENT OF THE REFERENCE	91
7.	MAKE CLEAR WHICH STATEMENT REFERENCES SUPPORT	91
8.	DO NOT COPY SOMEONE ELSE'S REFERENCES	91
9.	DO NOT CITE OUT-OF-DATE REFERENCES	91
10.	DO NOT BE IMPRESSED BY TOP JOURNALS	92
11.	DO NOT TRY TO RECONCILE CONFLICTING EVIDENCE	92
12.	ACTIVELY SEARCH FOR COUNTEREVIDENCE	92

HOW MANY REFERENCES IS ENOUGH? — 93
MORE ISN'T ALWAYS BETTER — 93
THE OTHER SIDE OF THE COIN — 94
GENERAL RECOMMENDATIONS — 94

CHAPTER 12: WRITING A LETTER TO THE EDITOR — 95

PICKING YOUR ACTING EDITOR AND SUGGESTING REVIEWERS — 95
WHAT'S INCLUDED IN A LETTER TO THE EDITOR? — 97
HOW DOES THIS WORK IN PRACTICE? — 97
WHY IS OUR PAPER SUITABLE FOR THIS JOURNAL? — 98
WHAT ARE OUR PAPER'S KEY CONTRIBUTIONS? — 98
ACTING EDITOR AND REVIEWERS — 99

CHAPTER 13: WHAT ELSE CAN YOU DO TO IMPROVE YOUR CHANCES? — 101

POLISH YOUR PAPER TO PERFECTION — 101
CANNOT AFFORD AN EDITOR OR PROOF-READER? — 102
GET YOUR NAME OR WORK KNOWN — 103
WHY IS ACADEMIC NETWORKING CRUCIAL? — 104
WHAT IS THAT CONFERENCE NETWORKING THING ABOUT? — 105
SOCIAL MEDIA NETWORKING — 107
GET A "FRIENDLY REVIEWER" AND TAKE R&Rs SERIOUSLY — 110

CONCLUSION — 111

FURTHER READING — 113

PUBLISHING — 113
CAREER PROGRESSION — 115
RESEARCH IMPACT AND FUNDING — 117
SOCIAL MEDIA — 119
OTHER ACADEMIC SKILLS — 120

Introduction

The first thing many PhD students and early career academics want to know is how to get their papers published, preferably in a good journal. I don't pretend to be the world's greatest expert on this, but I have published nearly 100 peer-reviewed articles since 1995, many of which in the top journals in my field. So, this short book documents the experience I have gathered over the years.

I focus on journal articles. This doesn't mean that other types of publications – such as books and book chapters – are unimportant. I have published quite a few of them myself, ranging from textbooks to research monographs, and from short practical guides (like this one) to contributions in edited volumes. However, publishing books and book chapters requires a very different skillset. I prefer to keep these guides focused.

My focus is on the field of Business & Management. However, most of my recommendations are equally applicable to the broader Social Sciences and to some extent to other disciplines too. This book is made up of two key parts:

- Getting started with paper writing. This includes chapters on the four Ps of publishing (Chapter 1), How to keep up to date with the literature (Chapter 2), Doing a literature review with the Publish or Perish software (Chapter 3), Finding out which journals publish on your topic (Chapter 4), and Targeting the right journal (Chapter 5).

- A structured approach to ensuring that your paper gets past the first hurdle in the peer review process: the desk-reject (Chapter 6). I focus on titles (Chapter 7), abstracts (Chapter 8), introductions (Chapter 9), conclusions (Chapter 10), using your references strategically (Chapter 11), writing a good letter to the editor (Chapter 12), and the other things you can do to improve your chances (Chapter 13).

I hope this book will help to demystify the topic of journal publishing and provides you with the necessary tools to be successful in your own publishing efforts. I would love to hear from you if it has. Feel free to get in touch with me at anne@harzing.com.

Note: This short guide is an edited and curated collection of my white papers and blogposts on the topic of publishing, published between 2010 and 2022.

Chapter 1:
The four Ps of publishing

Chapter 1 will start by providing you with a brief and – hopefully – memorable overview of what is important to be successful in the publishing process. For ease of recollection, I have taken a leaf from my Marketing colleagues and introduce the four Ps of publishing in top journals: perform, practice, participate, and persist.

Perform: submit the best paper you can

The first step to get your paper published in a top journal is that the paper itself is as good as possible. Top journals have high standards for theory development, research methods, rigour, originality of the contribution, and writing style.

Recognise your own limitations and be prepared to improve your skills through research training. Don't think that after you finish your PhD you never need to take another class again. As academics, we all need to engage in professional development throughout our careers.

Sometimes even professional development can't help us though; we all have our inherent strengths and weaknesses. And this is where collaboration comes in. If, for instance, theory building isn't your strength, but doing empirical work is, collaborate with others that have complementary skills.

You also need to really get to know the journal you are submitting to and ensure that your paper is the best it can be for *that* journal. Otherwise, you'll only end up with a desk-reject. A desk-reject means that your manuscript is rejected by a journal's editor without even being sent out for review.

In Chapters 6-13, we will discuss in more detail how you can ensure that your paper passes this first hurdle of the peer review process and is in with a chance to get constructive reviewer feedback.

Finally, make sure you never submit a paper to a journal without checking whether it publishes any articles on your topic at all. This is easy to do with the free Publish or Perish software that you can download from my website, www.harzing.com. We'll discuss this in more detail in Chapter 4.

Practice and see feedback as a gift

Just like any activity you will only get better at publishing with practice. Do ensure this practice is "guided", so you don't end up just repeating the same mistakes over and over again. Start playing the "publication game" when you are a PhD student. Try to learn as much as possible from your PhD supervisors. See developmental feedback on your work as a *gift* that helps you to improve it. Too many academics interpret constructive feedback as *critique* or even *discrimination* and become very defensive/argumentative.

There are many ways to get feedback on your paper. First, you can ask your colleagues to be a "friendly reviewer" and offer the same service in return. This means they read the paper as a reviewer would, but try to help you as much as possible. But don't rely on colleagues who just tell you: "*great paper, there is a typo on page 5*". Nice though it might be to hear your paper is perfect, this is hardly ever true. It just means that your colleagues can't be bothered to spend time on providing you with proper feedback.

Sending your paper off to conferences is also a good way to get feedback. Make sure though you submit to the *top* conferences in your field. With top conferences you can generally count on at least *one* rigorous review. If you are lucky, you might get several. Minor conferences accept papers with no or only very minimal reviewing.

Don't count on getting substantive feedback after your conference presentation, it's very hit and miss. In most cases you would be lucky to get *one* sensible comment; that's why written conference reviews are so important. That said, presenting at a conference is still important from a networking perspective (see the next section).

Getting your paper rejected after review is always disappointing. It is, however, a golden opportunity for useful feedback: you get to know what *real* reviewers think about the paper. This also means that you should never send out a rejected paper to another journal without making revisions first. Some of the feedback will be specific for the journal, inappropriate, or impossible to address. But there will *always* be some comments that are useful. So, do spend time revising the paper before sending it on to the next journal.

Participate in academic networks

You don't have to be the world's greatest networker or an exuberant extrovert to participate in academic networks. I am certainly not, quite the reverse in fact. However, do get out there and create your own academic networks. If you don't know where to start, consider volunteering! Volunteers are always in demand. You can volunteer to review for a conference or for academic journals, chair sessions at a conference, organise symposia or workshops, and to participate in committees of professional associations.

Networking will certainly not get a mediocre paper accepted, but it *may* make it easier for a good paper to get a chance. The top journals in many fields only accept 5-10% of the papers submitted. So, when an editor is in two minds about whether to offer the authors a chance to revise & resubmit, it can't hurt if they have clear positive associations with your name. After all, it is only human to have more confidence in people you know.

Despite the advent of social media, the best networking is still done face-to-face. So, whenever you have a chance, go to conferences. But make sure you *prepare*. Decide who you want to meet beforehand, don't just hang out with your friends. Try to meet someone new every time, and ask for introductions if necessary.

Also ensure that before you go to the conference you have prepared your research brief – a short summary about your research – in a few different versions:

- the 10-second elevator sound bite; this must be short as you don't want to be half-way when you reach the right floor ☺.
- the 1-minute coffee line version for when you are waiting in the queue at the coffee shop; can be expanded to the reception version depending on the length of the queue.
- the 2-3-minute reception version for when your counterpart is *really* interested.
- versions longer than 2-3 minutes are probably best suited for sit-down dinners with like-minded academics.

But most of all: Persist, Persist, Persist

If there is one characteristic that distinguishes successful academics from the less successful ones it is persistence. Don't give up! Rejection is part of an academic's daily life; if you would give up after a rejection you wouldn't get very far. So, try to get over rejection quickly and don't think it is personal; rejection might simply mean the journal wasn't the right outlet for your paper.

Use whatever is right for you to get the rejection out of your system: drinking wine, eating chocolate, a night out, moaning to colleagues, writing an angry response to the reviewers (without sending it!). Then just wait for a couple of days, read the rejection letter again – it will seem much more reasonable once you have cooled down – and revise the paper as soon as you can for another journal.

Don't think senior academics don't get rejections. My 2002 paper published in *Strategic Management Journal* was rejected at no less than three journals before it was accepted at SMJ. My 2002 paper in *Journal of Organizational Behavior* about academic referencing errors was desk-rejected ("doesn't fit the journal's mission") by nearly a dozen journal editors.

Over time you will get better at targeting your papers to the right journal. My own "hit rate" has certainly improved. However, even in the last 5 years I have still received nearly a dozen rejections. I can easily paper the walls with the rejections I have received in my 30-year career, and I would definitely need more than one room!

Chapter 2: How to keep up to date with the literature?

One of the first steps in writing up an academic article is keeping up with the literature and doing a literature review. So, this is what we will discuss in the next two chapters. After that we will talk about finding out which journals publish on your topic (Chapter 4) and targeting the right journal for your paper (Chapter 5).

A short history tour

In the "good old days" of the 1980s, the decade in which I did my own Bachelor's and Master's degrees, information overload wasn't much of a problem. At a time where study assignments were either handwritten or typed on an electric typewriter, keeping up to date with the literature consisted of browsing through the recent issues of academic journals. You could find these on display on the shelves of the library's reading room.

Tracking down references in academic articles involved making numerous trips to musty cellars of university libraries, sometimes even in other cities, and dragging large stacks of bound volumes to and from the photocopier. I still vividly remember the chemical smell of the thermal paper that was used in most photocopiers. I also spent looooots of time waiting patiently when someone else was using the photocopier, or cursing in desperation when a previous user had left it broken without alerting the technicians. Those were the days of (very) slow Science...

Things had "improved" slightly when I did my PhD. I now had my own personal computer and email started to become common as a means of communication, thus speeding up access to information. That said, much of my communication with other academics still took place via letters or – if you wanted "instant" communication - faxes, although their thermal paper became illegible after a while.

Despite the introduction of personal computers, keeping up to date with the literature still required visits to the library. To all intents and purposes, the Internet didn't really exist. In any case, dial-up modems and connections were so excruciatingly slow that getting the information from a book on the library shelves would usually be much quicker.

Drowning in information?

Fast forward 30 years or so and we are all at a risk of drowning in information. This is certainly true for many people's daily lives. Who would ever have thought that FOMO (Fear of Missing Out) would be the cause of serious mental health issues?

Personally, I don't "do" Facebook, Instagram, Snapchat, TikTok or whatever form of Social Media is the flavour of the month. I have absolutely no desire to broadcast my private life and, at the same time, help commercial companies collect and sell data about my consumption preferences. Nor for that matter am I very interested in the personal lives of others, beyond the small group of family and friends that I can easily keep in touch with without social media.

However, the risk of drowning is present in our professional lives too. You could literally spend all day trying to keep up to date with what is happening in your field. If you have online profiles on platforms such as ResearchGate, Academia.edu, Mendeley, Twitter, LinkedIn, and have enabled their email notifications, you could find your email inbox literally overflowing with alerts every single day.

For instance, one librarian I know joked that ResearchGate would send you an email whenever one of the academics in your network f*rted. I am following very few academics on ResearchGate and have disabled 95% of their alerts. This includes the follower alerts that tell you when someone reads or cites your paper, as well as the gratuitous "*you/your paper are/is the best*" type of alerts. Even so, I still get a few emails a week.

Social media alerts will provide you with low-quality information that only detracts your attention from any research you are working on. These alerts are tempting you to login again to check up on all the activity. This is fine if your intention is amusement, but not if it is to keep up to date with *serious* research. Scientific communication, especially in the Social Sciences, really is not so rapid that you need to ensure you get daily updates.

How to keep your head above the water?

That said, it would be foolish not to use these services to relieve the burden of keeping up to date in today's hectic academic world. So, my recommendations for keeping up to date with *important* new publications in your field would be as follows:

1. Set up citation alerts for your own articles

An article that cites one of your own articles has a high likelihood of being relevant to your research interests. Personally, I have found Google Scholar the best way to find out about articles citing my work. Despite its limitations, Google Scholar is still the most comprehensive source of citation data.

The easiest way to get citation alerts for your work is to set up a Google Scholar Citation Profile, which is easy and very quick to do. For guidance on this, see my blogposts "*Google Scholar Profiles: the good, the bad, and the better*", "*Social Media in Academia (3): Google Scholar Profiles*" and "*How to keep your Google Scholar Profile clean?*".

Once you have created a Google Scholar Profile you can create citation alerts for your entire body of work with just one click. This means Google Scholar will send you an email whenever one of your articles is cited. This includes a brief abstract of the article allows you to decide whether it is worth following up on. Most of the time you can even download a copy of the article there and then.

2. Set up new article alerts for other academics

If there are authors in your field that are crucial to your research, consider following them on Google Scholar. You can do this by searching for their Google Scholar Citation Profile and clicking on the follow button.

In this case, I would suggest you only follow their "new articles" and not their "new citations" as the latter might well flood your mailbox, especially if you follow several highly cited authors. Please note that you can achieve similar results by following academics on platforms like ResearchGate, but personally I find that information density is much higher for Google Scholar alerts.

3. Set up new article alerts for key topics in your field

If there is a particular topic that you would like to stay up to date with, simply conduct a search in Google Scholar and click on the "Create alert" link. This will send you email alerts whenever there is a new result for these search terms. I encourage you to make these searches as specific as possible to avoid being overwhelmed with a flood of barely relevant alerts.

4. Check Google Scholar's "my updates" regularly

Once you have set up a Google Scholar Citation Profile, Google Scholar will provide you with "my updates" alerts, their assessment of publications that might be of interest to you. These are based on your own publication history, as well any articles you have saved in GS's "my library". The more relevant articles you have in these two sources, the more relevant the alerts will be to you.

Reviewing these alerts would normally take only 10-15 minutes a month and I have found them to be pretty good. I am usually quite interested in one third of the suggestions and most of the remaining updates are of the "nice-to-know" type. I receive very few irrelevant updates.

5. Subscribe to Table of Contents alerts

In the "good old days", librarians would circulate folders with TOCs (tables of content) from relevant journals to academics. I still remember the pale-yellow manila folders with stacks of TOCs. They were often delayed for months, because a colleague lost them on their desk or went on a long holiday without passing the folder on to the next person on the list.

These days you can use the same "old fashioned" way to keep up to date by getting these TOC alerts by email. I do this by creating alerts in the Current Contents Connect of the Web of Science, which does work well. If you do not have access to the Web of Science, you could consider using the free service JournalTOCs.

6. Periodically review core journals in your field

Alerts sometimes come at inconvenient or busy times. So, oftentimes you may simply delete them without reading. Moreover, it is quite easy to miss some information even if you *do* look at the alerts.

So, several times a year, I take a few hours to manually review all the new issues of a list of core journals that I am interested in. I do this simply by logging in to my university library, searching for journal titles their A-Z journal list and reviewing the latest issues. This means that if an article is of interest, I can immediately download it for later reading.

In sum

Following these six steps I rarely miss an article that is important to me. As indicated above, and in more detail in Chapter 13, you can do much more than this by using social media to keep informed about academic developments.

However, if your goal is to keep up to date with relevant academic publications from a select group of journals and/or academics, I find the added value of these services to be low.

If rather than staying up to date with the literature you want to get an overview of all research in a particular area in the last 10 or 20 years, I recommend using the free Publish or Perish software to do a literature review. This is what we will turn to in the next chapter.

Chapter 3: Using Publish or Perish to do a literature review

To conduct a literature search in Google Scholar I recommend you use the Publish or Perish software, which you can download for free from my website. It also covers six other data sources.

Depending on how broad you want the results to be, you can either use a single word or multiple words. If you for instance quote the words "ethical marketing" or "workplace bullying", they will be matched in the order they were entered.

Publish or Perish allows you to use Boolean operators such as AND, OR, and NOT. You can use them to create more complex queries. For full details on this, refer to the Publish or Perish manual.

If you want to narrow down the results, use the **Title words** box. This search only provides publications with the words are included in the title. As you would expect important publications in a field to include relevant key words in their title, this might be a good strategy.

Comprehensive literature review:
Born global firms

Let's assume you would like to know what has been written about the concept of "born global" firms in the discipline of International Business. Born globals are firms who start operating internationally from their inception, rather than starting out as domestic firms first and only internationalising gradually.

To do so enter "born global" OR "born globals" in the **Title words** box. This results in more than 1000 papers, ten of which have been cited more than 1000 times.

Cites	Per ye...	R...	Authors	Title
h 4,290	238.33	18	GA Knight, ST Cavusgil	Innovation, organizational capabilities, and the born-global firm
h 2,922	584.40	11	TK Madsen, P Servais	The internationalization of born globals: an evolutionary proce...
h 2,674	102.85	5	G Knight, ST Cavusgil,...	The born global firm: a challenge to traditional internationaliza...
h 1,779	61.34	2	MW Rennie	Born global
h 1,461	97.40	38	L Zhou, W Wu, X Luo	Internationalization and the performance of born-global SMEs...
h 1,344	70.74	9	DD Sharma, A Blomste...	The internationalization process of born globals: a network view
h 1,221	81.40	46	J Weerawardena, GS M...	Conceptualizing accelerated internationalization in the born gl...
h 1,157	64.28	12	S Chetty, C Campbell-...	A strategic approach to internationalization: a traditional versu...
h 1,133	56.65	30	Ø Moen, P Servais	Born global or gradual global? Examining the export behavior...
h 1,051	150.14	35	ST Cavusgil, G Knight	The born global firm: An entrepreneurial and capabilities pers...

Founding authors

Sorting the results by year (just click on the column heading to do this) allows us to identify who the "founding author(s)" of the concept are. Below I have reproduced all articles with "born global" in the title until 2000; the first article was published in 1993 by Rennie in *McKinsey Quarterly*.

Cites	Per ye...	R...	Authors	Title	Year
h 1,779	61.34	2	MW Rennie	Born global	1993
h 115	4.11	1	ST Cavusgil, GA Knight	A quiet revolution in Australian exporters	1994
h 2,674	102.85	5	G Knight, ST Cavusgil,...	The born global firm: a challenge to traditional Internationali...	1996
56	2.24	1	ST Cavusgil, GA Knight	Explaining an emerging phenomenon for international marke...	1997
h 337	13.48	31	GA Knight	Emerging paradigm for international marketing: The born glo...	1997
65	2.71	6...	S Kandasaami	Internationalisation of small-and medium-sized born global f...	1998
5	0.22	2	P Servais, ES Rasmussen	Born Globals–connectors between various industrial districts	1999
4	0.17	6	C Gurau, A Ranchhod	The 'Born Global' Firms in UK Biotechnology	1999
h 346	15.73	23	TK Madsen, E Rasmuss...	Differences and similarities between born globals and other...	2000
h 171	7.77	65	E Autio, HJ Sapienza	Comparing process and born global perspectives in the inter...	2000
84	3.82	161	PD Harveston	Synoptic versus incremental internationalization: An examina...	2000
49	2.23	1...	T Almor	Born global: the case of small and medium sized, knowledge...	2000
29	1.32	217	G Knight, TK Madsen,...	The born global firm: description and empirical investigation...	2000
h 109	4.95	5...	J Bell, R McNAUGHTON	Born global firms: a challenge to public policy in support of i...	2000
56	2.55	6...	S Kandasaami, X Huang	International marketing strategy of SMEs: A comparison of b...	2000

The paper talks about a McKinsey study amongst Australian firms. It identified small and medium-sized companies that successfully competed against large, established players in the global arena without first building a home base. Thus, it appears a consulting firm in Australia has first discovered the born global phenomenon.

The second publication is an editorial by a well-known academic in International Marketing, who reports on the results of the McKinsey study that he discovered when spending 6 months as a Fulbright Scholar in Australia. Cavusgil (1994:4) says:

> *"I would like to comment on an interesting phenomenon in the Australian export scene. It is relevant to those of us in other post-industrial economies and, hopefully, should spur some research interests."*

The Australian angle is also apparent in a later conceptual paper published in 1998 by Kandasaami, University of Western Australia. Interestingly, this paper did gather a respectable 50 citations, despite being an unpublished working paper.

Historical development of the field

Our literature search also allows us to follow the development of this field of research over the decades. Cavusgil did take his own recommendation to heart and started researching this phenomenon, leading to a very highly cited publication in 1996 – co-authored with Gary Knight – in *Advances in International Marketing*. Knight and Cavusgil went on to publish many other papers in this field.

They were joined at an early stage by a Danish academic, Tage Madsen, who, with his Danish co-authors Servais and Rasmussen, also published several papers on the topic. In 1999, the phenomenon was also picked up in the UK, where Gurau & Ranchhod researched biotechnology firms.

By 2000 the topic had spread to researchers in the USA (Harveston et al.), Ireland (Bell), Finland (Autio), and Israel (Almor). Interest in it remained strong amongst researchers these countries, but after 2000 they were also joined by researchers in Sweden, Portugal, and New Zealand. Apart from a few researchers in the USA and Israel, the phenomenon initially attracted most interest from academics in "small" economies at the geographical peripheries of the world.

The mid 2000s saw the interest in the phenomenon expand to other countries such as Germany, Switzerland, Mexico, Korea, with Latin American countries (Brazil, Columbia, Costa Rica) and Italy joining from the late 2000s.

In the early 2010s the geographical interest had spread to India, China, and Eastern Europe. The year 2012 saw the publication of a *Handbook of Research on Born Globals* with 18 chapters by different researchers in the field, as well as an annotated bibliography.

In 2015, the 2014 JIBS award for the best paper of the decade went to Knight's and Cavusgil's paper *"Innovation, organizational capabilities, and the born-global firm"*. In the same year, Gary Knight published a review article (*"Born global firms: Evolution of a contemporary phenomenon"*) in *Advances in International Marketing*. It appears that after 20 years, the topic of "born globals" had reached maturity.

Since then, the field has blossomed with hundreds of publications since the mid 2010s. The field of born globals clearly continues to be of great interest to international business scholars. Scholars are now branching out into specialised topics such as born global family firms, as well as specific industries such as the music industry, natural cosmetics, and breweries.

Important journals

Sorting our results set on born global firms by journal (again just click on the column heading) allows us to identify the journals that have published articles relating to this topic.

It showed that all the mainstream international business journals (*Journal of International Business Studies*, *Journal of World Business*, *Management International Review*, and *International Business Review*) contain a substantial number of papers on the topic.

More specialized International Marketing journals such as *Journal of International Marketing* and *International Marketing Review* have also published many papers on this topic. Most of the born global firms are exporters rather than multinationals with subsidiaries abroad. Exporting is traditionally a topic of interest to the International Marketing community.

The results also showed many papers in the *International Journal of Globalisation and Small Business*, as well as a large number of papers in the *Journal of International Entrepreneurship*. This illustrates that the born global phenomenon often concerned small and medium-sized firms and thus that the early internationalization decision should be seen in the context of entrepreneurship.

Hence, our journal review has allowed us to identify not just the main outlets, but with them also the sub-disciplines in which this phenomenon has attracted substantive interest.

Follow up on key publications in the field

Your literature review will discover the seminal publications in the field. These could be either publications that are highly cited or publications that deal with exactly the topic you are interested in. Oftentimes, you will also want to ensure that you review papers that are citing this seminal piece of work. These papers might show up in your initial search, but if they look at the phenomenon from a slightly different angle and don't refer to the exact same concepts, they will not be captured.

So how can you use Publish or Perish to follow up on publications that cite your seminal publications? Simply right-click on the seminal article in question and chose "Lookup citations" in Publish or Perish. This will look up all publications referencing your seminal publication and present them ordered by the number of citations.

Cites	Per ye...	R...	Authors	Title
h 4,290	238.33	1	GA Knight, ST Cavusgil	Innovation, organizational capabilities, and the born-global firm
h 3,807	152.28	2	J Alba, J Lynch, B Weit...	Interactive home shopping: consumer, retailer, and manufacturer...
h 2,922	584.40	3	TK Madsen, P Servais	The internationalization of born globals: an evolutionary process?
h 1,811	120.73	4	JA Quelch, LR Klein	The Internet and international marketing
h 1,565	92.06	5	A Rialp, J Rialp, GA Kni...	The phenomenon of early internationalizing firms: what do we kn...
h 1,510	88.82	6	MV Jones, NE Coviello	Internationalisation: conceptualising an entrepreneurial process o...
h 1,461	97.40	7	L Zhou, W Wu, X Luo	Internationalization and the performance of born-global SMEs: th...
h 1,459	132.64	8	MV Jones, N Coviello,...	International entrepreneurship research (1989–2009): a domain...
h 1,344	70.74	9	DD Sharma, A Blomste...	The internationalization process of born globals: a network view
h 1,332	166.50	10	DJ Teece	A dynamic capabilities-based entrepreneurial theory of the multi...

19

The screenshot above shows the ten most highly cited articles that cite the first publication on born globals (Rennie 1996). Of these, four were already included in our initial search, as they have "born global" in the title. Of the remaining articles, the three articles by Alba et al., Quelch & Klein, and Teece are probably not very relevant. However, the publications by Rialp, Rialp & Knight and two articles by Jones & Coviello appear to be relevant, even though they do not mention the terms born global in the title.

In sum

Using Publish or Perish you can very quickly establish the seminal publications, founding authors, historical development, and important journal outlets of any field of research.

How to conduct a longitudinal literature review?

Publish or Perish can also be used to analyse the development of the literature on any topic longitudinally. You can search for specific key words and look at how the number of papers published varies over time. To eliminate many irrelevant results, it is a good idea to focus on a small set of journals. You can search for more than one journal at a time using the OR function in the publication field. Google Scholar limits the character count it accepts, so it will consider only the first three journals. Other data sources that can be accessed with Publish or Perish do not have such limitations.

Publish or Perish does not provide the ability to further analyse for instance the number of publications per year. However, exporting the data to a spreadsheet or statistical program allows you to do this very easily. Moreover, by selecting all publications in a given year, clicking "unselect" and looking at the reduction in the number of papers, you can quickly establish the number of papers per year.

Worked Example 1:
Culture in the field of International Business

Let us assume that you are interested in how research into the role of national culture in the field of International Business has developed over the years. To limit the number of irrelevant hits, you limit your search to the two mainstream International Business journals and use **Title words**. The screenshot below shows the search and all papers receiving more than 500 citations.

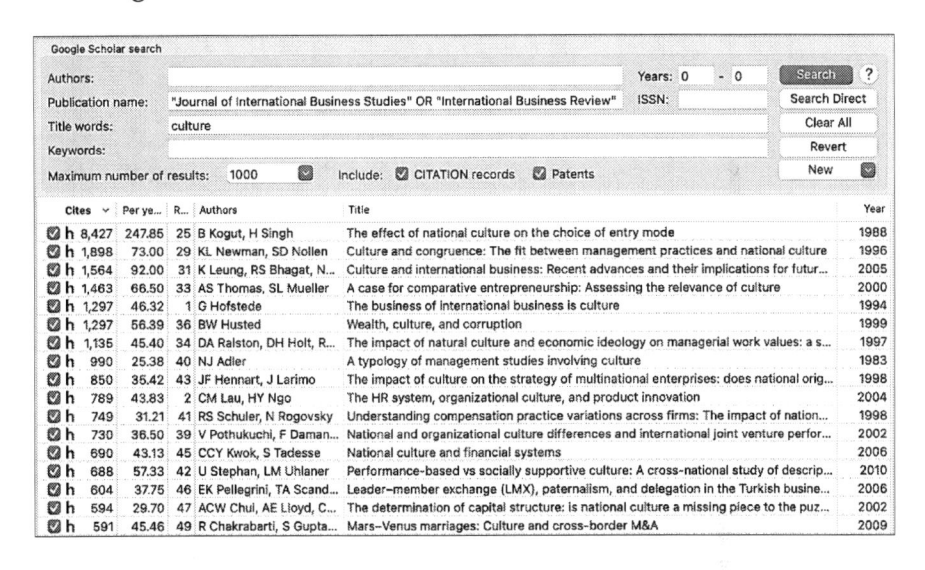

Cites	Per year	R...	Authors	Title	Year
h 8,427	247.85	25	B Kogut, H Singh	The effect of national culture on the choice of entry mode	1988
h 1,898	73.00	29	KL Newman, SD Nollen	Culture and congruence: The fit between management practices and national culture	1996
h 1,564	92.00	31	K Leung, RS Bhagat, N...	Culture and international business: Recent advances and their implications for futur...	2005
h 1,463	66.50	33	AS Thomas, SL Mueller	A case for comparative entrepreneurship: Assessing the relevance of culture	2000
h 1,297	46.32	1	G Hofstede	The business of international business is culture	1994
h 1,297	56.39	36	BW Husted	Wealth, culture, and corruption	1999
h 1,135	45.40	34	DA Ralston, DH Holt, R...	The impact of natural culture and economic ideology on managerial work values: a s...	1997
h 990	25.38	40	NJ Adler	A typology of management studies involving culture	1983
h 850	35.42	43	JF Hennart, J Larimo	The impact of culture on the strategy of multinational enterprises: does national orig...	1998
h 789	43.83	2	CM Lau, HY Ngo	The HR system, organizational culture, and product innovation	2004
h 749	31.21	41	RS Schuler, N Rogovsky	Understanding compensation practice variations across firms: The impact of nation...	1998
h 730	36.50	39	V Pothukuchi, F Daman...	National and organizational culture differences and international joint venture perfor...	2002
h 690	43.13	45	CCY Kwok, S Tadesse	National culture and financial systems	2006
h 688	57.33	42	U Stephan, LM Uhlaner	Performance-based vs socially supportive culture: A cross-national study of descrip...	2010
h 604	37.75	46	EK Pellegrini, TA Scand...	Leader-member exchange (LMX), paternalism, and delegation in the Turkish busine...	2006
h 594	29.70	47	ACW Chui, AE Lloyd, C...	The determination of capital structure: is national culture a missing piece to the puz...	2002
h 591	45.46	49	R Chakrabarti, S Gupta...	Mars-Venus marriages: Culture and cross-border M&A	2009

Highly cited papers and development over time

The most highly cited paper – by a large distance – is Kogut & Singh's paper on the effect of national culture on the choice of entry mode. This was a seminal paper because it introduced culture as a variable to be considered in entry mode studies. Other highly cited papers over the years are those providing reviews of the field (e.g., Adler in 1983, Hofstede in 1994, and Leung et al. in 2005).

21

However, the general study of the impact of culture on managerial work values and practices is also quite popular (Newman & Nollen; Ralston et al.). Further highly cited papers deal with the impact of culture on specific topics such as wealth and corruption (Husted), strategy (Hennart & Larimo), compensation practices (Schuler & Rogovsky), joint ventures (Pothukuchi et al.), financial systems (Kwok & Tadesse), capital systems (Chui) and mergers & acquisitions (Chakrabarti et al.). Inevitably, there are also a few articles that deal with organizational or business culture rather national culture (e.g. Lau & Ngo, Stephan & Uhlaner, and Pellegrini & Scandura).

By sorting the articles by year, I can establish that the interest in the role of culture is increasing. There were only six articles published in these two journals the 1980s that had culture in their title. Likewise, in the first half of the nineties, there were only five articles that dealt with culture to such an extent that they included the word in their title. In the latter half of the nineties, the total number of articles had increased to nearly a dozen.

The first decade of the 21st century produced some 40 articles in JIBS and IBR with the word culture in the title, with another 50-odd published in the next decade. Culture is definitely a topic that appears to be of sustained interest to international business scholars!

Worked example 2:
HIV in Science, Nature, and Cell

Note: all searches in this section were conducted in 2015. Current results might differ, but the basic principles remain the same.

Let us assume that you are interested in how research on HIV has developed over the years. You focus your search only on three core journals that are most likely to publish on this topic: *Science*, *Nature*, and *Cell*. The screenshot below shows all papers with more than 2,500 citations.

We can see that each of the three journals has published highly cited articles in this field: two in *Cell*, five in *Nature* and five in *Science*. We can also observe that most of the highly cited articles on this topic were published between 1995 and 1998, and in fact 9 out of the 12 most highly cited articles were published in 1996.

Cites	Per year	Authors	Title	Year	Publication
h 4675	212.50*	DD Ho, AU Neumann, AS Perelson, W Chen	Rapid turnover of plasma virions and CD4 lymphocy...	1995	Nature
h 3958	188.48*	HK Deng, R Liu, W Ellmeier, S Choe	Identification of a major co-receptor for primary isol...	1996	Nature
h 3479	165.67*	T Dragic, V Litwin, GP Allaway	HIV-1 entry into CD4 plus cells is mediated by the ch...	1996	Nature
h 3397	161.76*	AS Perelson, AU Neumann, M Markowitz...	HIV-1 dynamics in vivo: virion clearance rate, infecte...	1996	Science
h 3133	142.41*	F Cocchi, AL DeVico, A Garzino-Demo, SK Arya	Identification of RANTES, MIP-1alpha, and MIP-1bet...	1995	Science
h 3048	145.14*	G Alkhatib, C Combadiere, CC Broder, Y Feng	CC CKR5: A RANTES, MIP-1alpha, MIP-1beta recept...	1996	Science
h 2977	156.68*	PD Kwong, R Wyatt, J Robinson, RW Sweet, J Sodr...	Structure of an HIV gp120 envelope glycoprotein in ...	1998	Nature
h 2960	140.95*	R Liu, WA Paxton, S Choe, D Ceradini, SR Martin...	Homozygous defect in HIV-1 coreceptor accounts f...	1996	Cell
h 2863	136.33*	M Samson, F Libert, BJ Doranz, J Rucker	Resistance to HIV-1 infection in caucasian individual...	1996	Nature
h 2843	135.38*	JW Mellors, CR Rinaldo Jr, P Gupta, RM White	Prognosis in HIV-1 infection predicted by the quanti...	1996	Science
h 2533	120.62*	M Dean, M Carrington, C Winkler, GA Huttley	Genetic restriction of HIV-1 infection and progressio...	1996	Science
h 2499	119.00*	H Choe, M Farzan, Y Sun, N Sullivan, B Rollins...	The β-chemokine receptors CCR3 and CCR5 facilitat...	1996	Cell

Development of research volume over time

However, I am also interested in how the volume of research on HIV has developed over the years. To assess this, I have rerun the search for a single journal only: *Science*. The reason for this is that if I include all journals only the most highly cited 1,000 results will be shown, as Google Scholar limits its results to 1,000. This will naturally include fewer recent articles as they are not yet highly cited.

I also split my search into two time periods and then aggregated both searches into one. This ensured that I also included less-cited articles (there are more than 100 articles without any citations in both periods). This reduces the risk of missing most of the recently published articles. In doing so I was able to conclude the following.

- **The number of publications on HIV peaked in 1988:** When I sort the results by year, I find that articles on HIV started to be published in Science in 1986. However, after removing duplicates, I found only four articles published in that year. About a dozen articles were published in 1987, whilst nearly 50 articles were published in 1988. This was the year with the largest number of publications on HIV in *Science*.

23

- **Another peak in publications appeared in 1996:** Between 1989 and 1995 the number of articles had gone down to about 20-30. However, in 1996 the number of articles reached nearly 50 again, dropping to around 30 again in 1997-1999. Then, from the early 2000s, the number of articles published went down to about 15 a year, with a seeming resurgence from 2013 onwards where we see a return to 25-30 articles a year.

It appears publication peaks follow major medical developments. The name HIV was introduced in May 1986 by the International Committee on the Taxonomy of Viruses. The current treatment for HIV was introduced in 1996, resulting in a declining number of deaths from HIV/AIDS. So, by studying the scientific interest in HIV (or any illness) through journal publications, we can understand the development of interest in the disease over time.

So, we are now familiar with the best strategies to keep up to date with the literature and how to review it using the Publish or Perish software. This will help you in writing up your paper. The next step though is to decide where to submit your paper. This is what we will focus on in the next two chapters.

In Chapter 4, I will show you how to use Publish or Perish to find which journals publish articles on your topic. In Chapter 5, we will then discuss the importance of carefully targeting the right journal, including a discussion on how to avoid predatory journals.

Chapter 4: Where to submit your paper?

Let's assume you have written a paper, but are still unsure which journal to submit it to. Normally, you would already have a good idea of suitable journals through your literature review, but there might be good reasons why you haven't been able to settle on a journal yet.

- You might want to ensure you haven't neglected any options.

- You might already know what the most suitable journal for your paper would be, but you have already published several papers there, and are keen to show the impact of your work beyond your immediate academic peer group.

- The most appropriate journal is one where you have recently had a bad experience in the review process (e.g., long delays or shoddy reviewer reports).

Use Publish or Perish to search for keywords

What you can do in this case is use Publish or Perish to conduct a search with the most important keywords in your paper. If you search for a relatively generic topic, many of the hits you get will be books, especially in the Social Sciences and Humanities. Books tend to be highly cited because they contain more citable material than short journal articles. This is especially true for classic works in the field.

Sort the results by publication outlet

We are not currently intending to write a book. So, the best way to find appropriate journals is to sort the results by publication outlet. Do this by clicking on the Publication column. The default sort for Publish or Perish is the number of citations. So, by clicking on the Publication column you will create a list sorted by publication outlet first and then by the number of citations. Scrolling down the list you can easily identify the journals that contain articles on your topic. It also shows us which of these articles are most highly cited.

Worked example: Ethical marketing

Let's assume you have written a paper about ethical marketing. During your literature review, you have already noticed that the top mainstream marketing journals such as the *Journal of Marketing* and *Journal of Consumer Research* do not seem to publish a lot of papers on this topic. Hence, you are looking for alternative options. To achieve this, use the Publish or Perish software and follow these two simple steps:

1. **Use the quoted terms in the keywords box**. Enter the words *ethical marketing* in the **Keywords** box. This will result in articles in which the two words *ethical marketing* appear in that order. If you include the search term *ethical marketing* without quotes it will provide many more matches as it matches the words in any order. There will be lots of publications that include both these relatively generic words.

2. **Limit the search to recent years**. As you want to ensure that the journal has published on ethical marketing in recent years, you limit the search to the last decade. This particular search was conducted in 2010. Hence, the results found range between 2000 and 2010.

The search resulted in 874 hits. As expected, many of the most-cited works are books, often generic ones on Marketing Research, Consumer Behaviour, and International Marketing. However, sorting the results by publication allows us to identify the most important journal outlets. Below, you will find screenshots with the most frequently occurring journals in this search, with a brief discussion of the results for each.

Journal of Business Ethics

The *Journal of Business Ethics* is by far the most frequently mentioned journal in our search. The screenshot below shows some of the most cited papers.

Title	Year	Publication
A review of empirical studies assessing ethical decision making in business	2000	Journal of Business Ethics
A cross cultural comparison of the contents of codes of ethics: USA, Canada and ...	2000	Journal of Business Ethics
Unpacking the ethical product	2001	Journal of Business Ethics
A partnership model of corporate ethics	2002	Journal of Business Ethics
Cross-cultural methodological issues in ethical research	2000	Journal of Business Ethics
An empirical investigation of the relationships between ethical beliefs, ethical ideo...	2001	Journal of Business Ethics
Ethics in personal selling and sales management: a review of the literature focusi...	2000	Journal of Business Ethics
An ethical exploration of privacy and radio frequency identification	2005	Journal of Business Ethics
Ethics and Marketing on this Internet: Practitioners' Perceptions of Societal, Indu...	2000	Journal of Business Ethics
The questionable use of moral development theory in studies of business ethics: ...	2001	Journal of Business Ethics
Packaging ethics: Perceptual differences among packaging professionals, brand ...	2000	Journal of Business Ethics
International marketing ethics from an Islamic perspective: a value-maximization ...	2001	Journal of Business Ethics
Gender differences in ethical perceptions of salespeople: An empirical examinatio...	2002	Journal of Business Ethics
Ethical judgment and whistleblowing intention: examining the moderating role of l...	2003	Journal of Business Ethics
Is cross-cultural similarity an indicator of similar marketing ethics?	2001	Journal of Business Ethics

Even though there are a few papers relating to marketing, most of the papers seem to deal mostly with general business ethics. Even so, this could be an option for Marketing academics who want to reach out to a more general audience interested in ethics.

Journal of Macromarketing

The second most frequently listed journal in our search is *Journal of Macromarketing*. The screenshot below shows all the hits in order of the number of citations.

Title	Year	Publication
The general theory of marketing ethics: a revision and three questions	2006	Journal of macromarketing
Normative perspectives for ethical and socially responsible marketing	2006	Journal of Macromarketing
Building understanding of the domain of consumer vulnerability	2005	Journal of Macromarketing
Quality-of-life (QOL) marketing: Proposed antecedents and consequences	2004	Journal of Macromarketing
Macro measures of consumer well-being (CWB): a critical analysis and a researc...	2006	Journal of Macromarketing
Globalization and technological achievement: Implications for macromarketing an...	2004	Journal of Macromarketing
Research on marketing ethics: A systematic review of the literature	2007	Journal of Macromarketing
Distributive justice: Pressing questions, emerging directions, and the promise of ...	2008	Journal of Macromarketing
Research on consumer well-being (CWB): Overview of the field and introduction...	2007	Journal of Macromarketing
The small and long view	2006	Journal of Macromarketing
Voluntary codes of ethical conduct: Group membership salience and globally inte...	2007	Journal of Macromarketing
On Economic Growth, Marketing Systems, and the Quality of Life	2009	Journal of Macromarketing
Assessing distributive justice in marketing: a benefit-cost approach	2007	Journal of Macromarketing
Globalization, transformation, and quality of life: Reflections on ICMD-8 and par...	2004	Journal of Macromarketing
Limited choice: An exploratory study into issue items and soldier subjective well-...	2006	Journal of Macromarketing
Handbook of Quality-of-Life Research: An Ethical Marketing Perspective, by M. ...	2003	Journal of Macromarketing
Applying Catholic Social Teachings to Ethical Issues in Marketing	2009	Journal of Macromarketing
Medicalization and Marketing	2010	Journal of Macromarketing

This journal has published a range of highly cited papers in this field and as such might be an appropriate outlet. However, many of the articles seems to focus on high-level societal issues, quality of life or consumer well-being. This is also reflected in the journal's editorial statement. Whether or not this suits your paper obviously depends on its topic.

> *"The Journal of Macromarketing examines important social issues, how they are affected by marketing, and how society influences the conduct of marketing."*

European Journal of Marketing

The journal that had the third largest number of hits for the search with the keywords "ethical marketing" was the *European Journal of Marketing*. The screenshot below shows all resulting papers in order of number of citations. Unfortunately, Google Scholar sometimes does abbreviate the title of a journal (see the first five hits).

Title	Year	Publication
How important are ethics and social responsibility?	2001	European Journal of ...
Moral philosophies of marketing managers	2002	European Journal of ...
An ethical basis for relationship marketing: a virtue ethics perspective	2007	European journal of ...
Corporate social responsibility: investigating theory and research in the marke...	2008	European Journal of ...
Children's impact on innovation decision making	2009	European Journal of ...
Grounded theory, ethnography and phenomenology	2005	European journal of Marketing
Societal marketing and morality	2002	European Journal of Marketing
Marketing as a profession: on closing stakeholder gaps	2002	European Journal of Marketing
Futures dilemmas for marketers: can stakeholder analysis add value?	2005	European Journal of Marketing
Ethics and value creation in business research: comparing two approaches	2006	European Journal of Marketing
An ethical basis for relationship marketing: a virtue ethics perspective The Aut...	2007	European Journal of Marketing

This means that the citation order is not perfect as it starts again with the first article for the non-abbreviated journal title, i.e., the *"Grounded theory, ethnography..."* article has more citations than most of the preceding articles. However, as we are mainly interested in finding journal outlets rather than doing a citation analysis, this is not a serious problem.

Perusing the titles, the *European Journal of Marketing* appears to have a rather broad focus, publishing papers in a variety of areas in marketing. Indeed, this is reflected in its mission statement:

> *"We welcome novel and ground-breaking contributions from a wide range of research traditions within the broad domain of marketing".*

This statement also mentions:

> *"The EJM is receptive to controversial topics, and new, as well as developments that challenge existing theories and paradigms."*

Hence, at first glance, this might not be a bad outlet for a topic that is not yet part of the mainstream in Marketing.

Journal of Consumer Marketing

As shown in the screenshot below, *Journal of Consumer Marketing* has also published a substantial number of papers containing the key words ethical marketing in the past decade. Not surprisingly, most of these papers focus on the ethical consumer. Hence, this journal would be a very appropriate outlet if your paper is focusing on the ethical aspects of consumer behaviour.

Title	Year	Publication
Shopping for a better world? An interpretive study of the potential for ethical...	2004	Journal of Consumer ...
"To legislate or not to legislate": a comparative exploratory study of privacy...	2003	Journal of consumer ...
An inquiry into the ethical perceptions of sub-cultural groups in the US: Hispa...	2002	Journal of Consumer ...
Consumers' Rules of Engagement in Online Information Exchanges	2009	Journal of Consumer ...
The myth of the ethical consumer-do ethics matter in purchase behaviour?	2001	Journal of consumer marketing
The ethicality of altruistic corporate social responsibility	2002	Journal of Consumer Marketing
Consumer privacy and the Internet in Europe: a view from Germany	2003	Journal of Consumer Marketing
Neuromarketing: a layman's look at neuroscience and its potential application...	2007	Journal of Consumer Marketing

Journal of Public Policy & Marketing

Another journal with a fairly large number of papers on this topic is *Journal of Public Policy & Marketing*. Perusing the article titles, its topics appear to have some overlap with the *Journal of Macromarketing*.

Title	Year	Publication
Does Fair Trade deliver on its core value proposition? Effects on income, e...	2009	Journal of Public Policy & ...
The philosophy and methods of deliberative democracy: Implications for p...	2009	Journal of Public Policy & ...
Marketing to the Poor: An Integrative Justice Model for Engaging Impoveri...	2009	Journal of Public Policy & ...
Consumer online privacy: legal and ethical issues	2000	Journal of Public Policy & Marketing
Antiglobal challenges to marketing in developing countries: Exploring the id...	2005	Journal of Public Policy & Marketing
Ethics and Public Policy Implications of Research on Consumer Well-Being	2008	Journal of Public Policy & Marketing
Principle-Based Stakeholder Marketing: Insights from Private Triple-Bottom...	2010	Journal of Public Policy & Marketing
Ethical Beliefs and Information Asymmetries in Supplier Relationships	2010	Journal of Public Policy & Marketing

This is confirmed when we look at its editorial statement:

> *"Journal of Public Policy & Marketing has adopted the noteworthy mission of publishing thoughtful articles on how marketing practice shapes and is shaped by societally important factors such as ..."*

Hence it appears that these two journals would be particularly appropriate if your paper focused on the societal issues surrounding ethical marketing.

Journal of Marketing Education

A surprising discovery was the realisation that the *Journal of Marketing Education* had published a fairly large number of papers in this area. Hence, if your paper had clear links to marketing education, or was investigating perceptions of marketing students, this might be an appropriate outlet for your article.

Title	Year	Publication
The effects of marketing education and individual cultural values on marketing...	2002	Journal of Marketing Education
Important factors underlying ethical intentions of students: Implications for m...	2004	Journal of Marketing Education
The Impact of Corporate Culture, the Reward System, and Perceived Moral I...	2005	Journal of Marketing Education
Teaching marketing law: A business law perspective on integrating marketing ...	2000	Journal of Marketing Education
Designing discussion activities to achieve desired learning outcomes: Choices ...	2007	Journal of Marketing Education
Group-Based Assessment as a Dynamic Approach to Marketing Education	2009	Journal of Marketing Education

Journal of the Academy of Marketing science

In your literature review you already discovered that the mainstream marketing journals have not published that many articles in ethical marketing. It should, therefore, come as a pleasant surprise to see that *Journal of the Academy of Marketing Science*, one of the top mainstream marketing journals, has published four articles on the topic between 2000 and 2010.

Title	Year	Publication
Representing the perceived ethical work climate among marketing employ...	2000	Journal of the Academy of ...
Consumer online privacy concerns and responses: a power-responsibility...	2007	Journal of the Academy of Marketing
Marketing with integrity: ethics and the service-dominant logic for marketing	2008	Journal of the Academy of Marketing.
A simulation of moral behavior within marketing exchange relationships	2007	Journal of the Academy of Marketing.

31

Its editorial statement indicates that articles in a very broad range of topics are acceptable, including ethics and social responsibility. Hence, if you judge your article to be of sufficient quality to merit publication in one of the top journals in marketing, this might be an appropriate choice. It would allow you to reach the widest possible audience in the broad field of marketing.

Using the "title words" box to further refine results

Judging from the titles in the results shown above, some articles didn't really seem to have a major focus on ethical marketing, but instead simply mentioned the words somewhere in the article.

Another option, therefore, would be to narrow down your results by using the **Title words** box. The results will only contain articles that have the words ethical marketing in their title, although the words do not necessarily appear close together. The screenshot below produces the results in order of the number of citations.

Title	Year	Publication
Normative perspectives for ethical and socially responsible marketing	2006	Journal of Macromarketing
Representing the perceived ethical work climate among marketing employees	2000	Journal of the Academy of ...
Important factors underlying ethical intentions of students: Implications for ma...	2004	Journal of Marketing Education
Perceived risk, moral philosophy and marketing ethics: mediating influences on ...	2002	Journal of Business research
Ethical guidelines for marketing practice: A reply to Gaski & some observations ...	2001	Journal of Business Ethics
Consumer interests and the ethical implications of marketing: a contingency fra...	2003	Journal of Consumer Affairs
Ethical marketing for competitive advantage on the internet	2001	Academy of Marketing Science
The Impact of Corporate Culture, the Reward System, and Perceived Moral In...	2005	Journal of Marketing Education
An ethical basis for relationship marketing: a virtue ethics perspective	2007	European journal of ...
Ethical trends in marketing and psychological research	2001	Ethics & Behavior
Sustainable Tourism: Ethical Alternative or Marketing Ploy?	2007	Journal of business ethics
The impact of cultural values on marketing ethical norms: A study in India and t...	2006	Journal of International ...

Comparing the journal titles with our previous results shows that most of the same journals appear in the list. However, there are five new journals that appear on the scene: *Journal of Business Research, Academy of Marketing Science Review, Journal of Consumer Affairs, Ethics & Behavior,* and *Journal of International Marketing*. These journals did not feature on our list before as they only published one or two papers on ethical marketing. However, if the titles appear relevant to your paper, they might be worth considering.

Review key academics in your field

Another good option to establish which journals are important in your field of study is to look up established academics in your field. The reasoning here is that if successful academics in your field have published in these journals, there is a high likelihood that these journals are appropriate outlets for your own work too.

Below, I have reproduced a Publish or Perish Google Scholar Profile search for two academics who are working in the broader field of "Marketing in society" or "responsible/sustainable marketing".

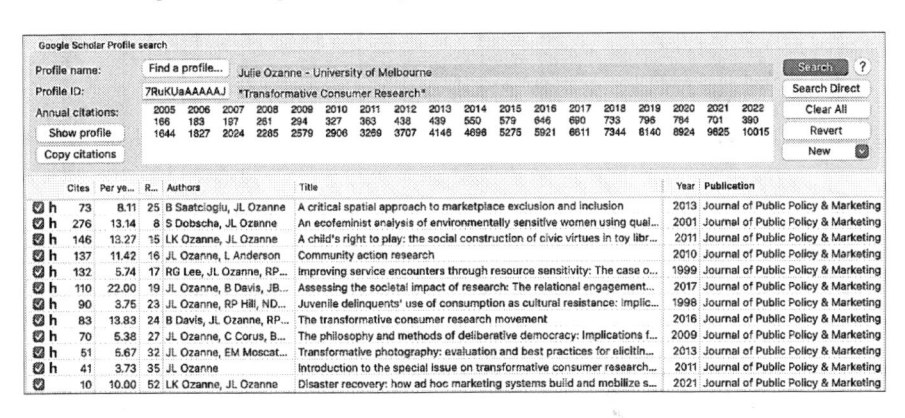

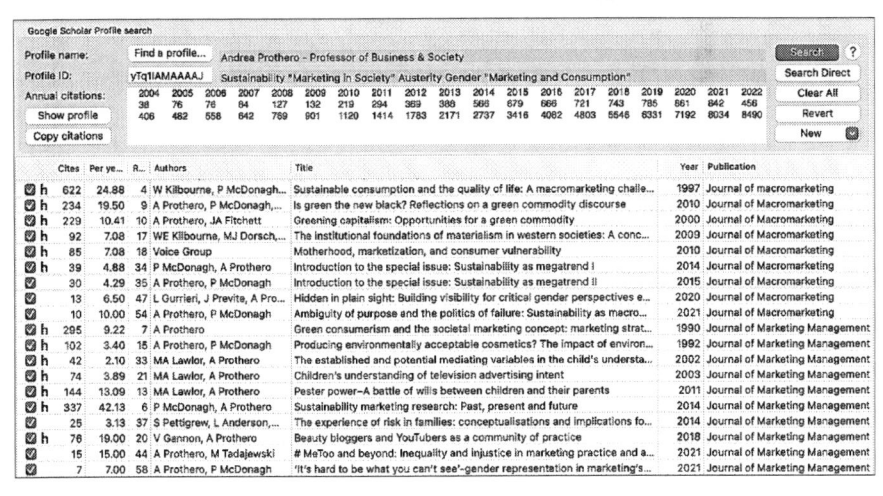

The two journals that we identified earlier in this chapter as being particularly appropriate outlets for marketing articles focusing on broader societal issues – *Journal of Public Policy & Marketing* and *Journal of Macromarketing* – both feature in the publication lists of these academics. Hence, this provides additional reassurance that these journals might be a good outlet for your paper.

However, we can also see that a journal that had not yet come up in our earlier keywords searches – *Journal of Marketing Management* – is a popular outlet for one of the academics for a ranges of responsible marketing topics. She has published multiple articles in this journal from 1990 onwards. This includes two papers in 2021, indicating that this journal's mission hasn't changed in this respect as is confirmed by its current mission statement.

> *"The JMM explicitly desires to see all paradigmatic traditions contribute to debates on marketing theory and practice. This includes traditional, predominantly managerial contributions aligned with logical empiricist perspectives, through to interpretive and Consumer Culture Theoretic (CCT) reflections on marketing's role in providing the resources for identity building and self-affirmation, as well as the negative ramifications of consumption on individuals and communities. Studies that engage with both the light-side and dark-side of marketing and consumer practice are welcome.*
>
> *Going beyond these two research orientations, the JMM seeks to support a number of other important paradigmatic traditions including Marxist and Neo-Marxist perspectives, postmodern interpretations of marketing and consumer practice, postcolonial understandings, macromarketing and Transformative Consumer Research (TCR) interventions, to name just a few which further marketing thought. The paradigmatic pluralism of the JMM is underwritten by a belief that marketing scholarship must be theoretically embedded and reflexive if it is to enhance our knowledge of marketing theory and practice(s)."*

Before submission:
Have you missed any papers?

Before submitting to a journal, use the Publish or Perish software to find out whether the journal you intend to submit to has published any (recent) relevant papers on your topic. You might have missed them whilst working hard on the final version of your paper. Few things that annoy a journal editor more than receiving a paper for their journal that neglects to refer to relevant papers in the journal in question. I am not talking here about the practice of less scrupulous journal editors who are asking you to cite papers from their own journal simply to increase their journal's ISI Journal Impact Factor.

However, journal editors are rightly annoyed if you have failed to incorporate **relevant** prior papers from their journal. By publishing in a certain journal, you are contributing to a conversation. And not acknowledging the other conversation partners is plain rude. So how do you do a final check to establish that you haven't missed any highly relevant papers in the journal you are targeting? You could simply browse tables of contents on the web or in the library. However, Publish or Perish offers a much quicker way.

Worked example: Entry modes of Japanese MNCs

Let's assume you have written a paper about entry mode choice (the choice between different ways to enter a foreign market) of Japanese multinational companies and intend to submit to *Journal of International Business Studies*. Simply search for the term "entry mode" (in quotes) in the **Keyword** field of the with "*Journal of International Business Studies*" in the **Publication** field. This will provide any articles in which the words *entry mode* appear in that order. The screenshot below provides **all** articles that have been published in *Journal of International Business Studies* since its inception in 1970 that have entry mode in their title, sorted by number of citations, a total of no less than 600 papers. Note I have unclicked the [citations] box to reduce the number of "stray citations".

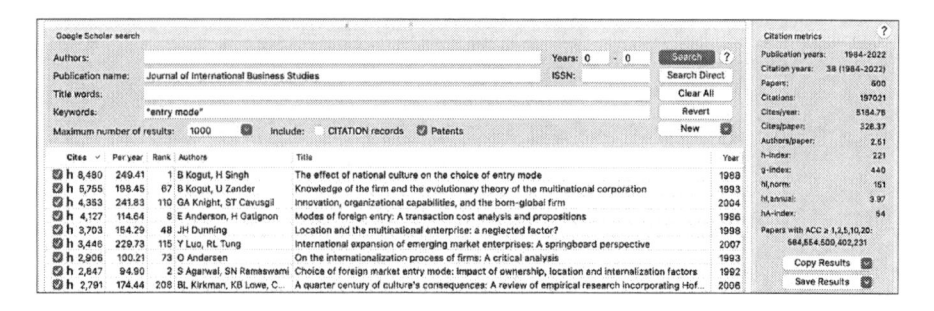

As Google Scholar matches keywords anywhere in the article, this search provides you with far too many results to cope with. So, you can narrow down your search in three ways:

1. Using a data source that searches only in the title and abstract, such as the Web of Science. However, this will still provide you with 134 results.
2. Limit the search to the last 10 years only. However, this will still provide you with 298 results for Google Scholar and 62 results for the Web of Science.
3. Search in the **Title words** box instead. Combined with the last 10-year criterion, this leads to a very manageable 12 papers (see screenshot below).

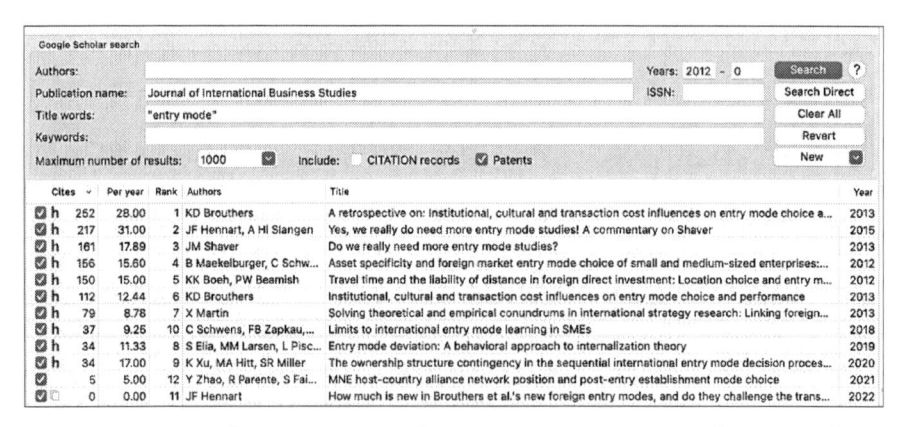

As you can see there is even a discussion going on in the journal on whether more research on entry mode is needed, something you might like to refer to in your paper. If you wanted to double-check whether you missed any papers dealing with Japan, you could relax the last 10 years criterion and search for Japan in the keyword field. Using Google Scholar, you would also be able to capture papers that mentioned Japan in the main text of the article only (see below).

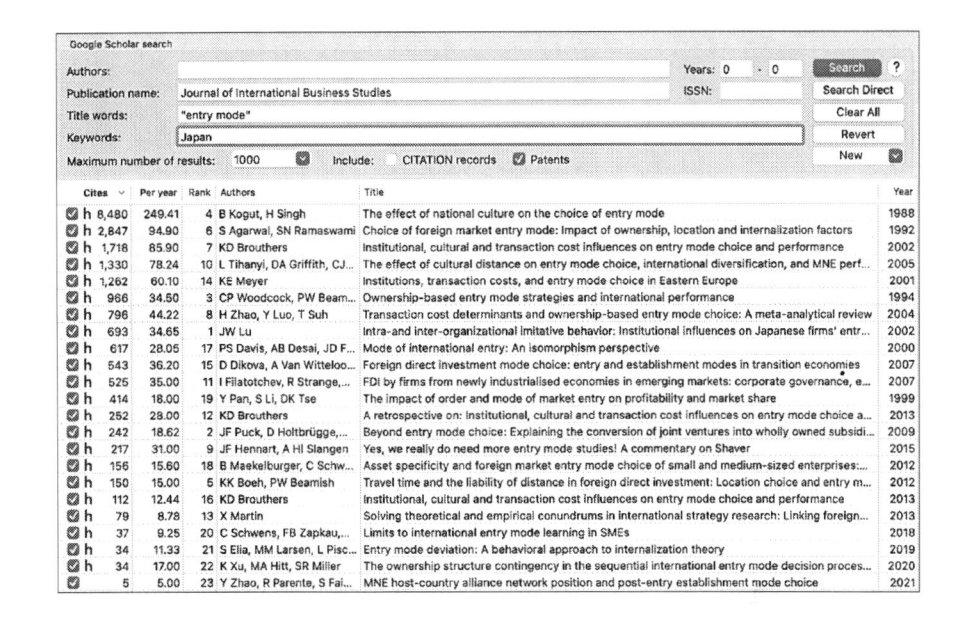

	Cites	Per year	Rank	Authors	Title	Year
☑ h	8,480	249.41	4	B Kogut, H Singh	The effect of national culture on the choice of entry mode	1988
☑ h	2,847	94.90	6	S Agarwal, SN Ramaswami	Choice of foreign market entry mode: Impact of ownership, location and internalization factors	1992
☑ h	1,718	85.90	7	KD Brouthers	Institutional, cultural and transaction cost influences on entry mode choice and performance	2002
☑ h	1,330	78.24	10	L Tihanyi, DA Griffith, CJ...	The effect of cultural distance on entry mode choice, international diversification, and MNE perf...	2005
☑ h	1,262	60.10	14	KE Meyer	Institutions, transaction costs, and entry mode choice in Eastern Europe	2001
☑ h	966	34.50	2	CP Woodcock, PW Beam...	Ownership-based entry mode strategies and international performance	1994
☑ h	796	44.22	8	H Zhao, Y Luo, T Suh	Transaction cost determinants and ownership-based entry mode choice: A meta-analytical review	2004
☑ h	693	34.65	1	JW Lu	Intra-and inter-organizational imitative behavior: Institutional influences on Japanese firms' entr...	2002
☑ h	617	28.05	17	PS Davis, AB Desai, JD F...	Mode of international entry: An isomorphism perspective	2000
☑ h	543	36.20	15	D Dikova, A Van Witteloo...	Foreign direct investment mode choice: entry and establishment modes in transition economies	2007
☑ h	525	35.00	11	I Filatotchev, R Strange,...	FDI by firms from newly industrialised economies in emerging markets: corporate governance, e...	2007
☑ h	414	18.00	19	Y Pan, S Li, DK Tse	The impact of order and mode of market entry on profitability and market share	1999
☑ h	252	28.00	12	KD Brouthers	A retrospective on: Institutional, cultural and transaction cost influences on entry mode choice a...	2013
☑ h	242	18.62	2	JF Puck, D Holtbrügge,...	Beyond entry mode choice: Explaining the conversion of joint ventures into wholly owned subsidi...	2009
☑ h	217	31.00	9	JF Hennart, A HI Slangen	Yes, we really do need more entry mode studies! A commentary on Shaver	2015
☑ h	156	15.60	18	B Maekelburger, C Schw...	Asset specificity and foreign market entry mode choice of small and medium-sized enterprises:...	2012
☑ h	150	15.00	5	KK Boeh, PW Beamish	Travel time and the liability of distance in foreign direct investment: Location choice and entry m...	2012
☑ h	112	12.44	16	KD Brouthers	Institutional, cultural and transaction cost influences on entry mode choice and performance	2013
☑ h	79	8.78	13	X Martin	Solving theoretical and empirical conundrums in international strategy research: Linking foreign...	2013
☑ h	37	9.25	20	C Schwens, FB Zapkau,...	Limits to international entry mode learning in SMEs	2018
☑ h	34	11.33	21	S Elia, MM Larsen, L Pisc...	Entry mode deviation: A behavioral approach to internalization theory	2019
☑ h	34	17.00	22	K Xu, MA Hitt, SR Miller	The ownership structure contingency in the sequential international entry mode decision proces...	2020
☑	5	5.00	23	Y Zhao, R Parente, S Fai...	MNE host-country alliance network position and post-entry establishment mode choice	2021

No papers at all?

If your search finds that the journal you intend to submit your paper to has **never** published anything on the topic of your paper or has last published something more than a decade ago, you might need to think again about your choice. Remember: wanting to submit to the journal, because it is the top-ranked journal in your field, is not a good enough reason!

Of course, there can be good reasons to want to introduce a particular stream of research to a new audience but realise that this is not an easy way to get your paper accepted. Just like people in general, academics often find it difficult to relate to ideas that have no connection at all to their knowledge base. For more details on the importance of contributing to the conversation, see Chapter 5.

If there is no prior published work on your topic in the journal, reviewers of the journal might not be familiar with this field and might not be able to evaluate its merits. It might also mean that the readers of the journal might not be interested in reading your work, even if it should get accepted. Maybe it is a sign you should take a step back and examine which journals publish on your topic?

Conclusion

Publish or Perish allows you to quickly get a very comprehensive overview of the journals that might be appropriate outlets for your next paper. Give it a try for your next paper and let me know how you fare. In the next chapter I'll discuss the importance of targeting your article to the right journal.

Chapter 5: Who do you talk to? Targeting journals

The first, and most important, step in maximising your publication chances is choosing your target journal very carefully. By far the most common reason for rejection is that your paper simply doesn't fit the journal. Sometimes, this lack of fit is "absolute", an empirical paper for instance will never be accepted for a conceptual journal and vice-versa.

Oftentimes, however, this lack of fit is created by authors who do not connect properly with the journal's *conversation*. For an excellent and extended discussion on this, refer to Anne Huff's book *"Writing for Scholarly Publication"*.

By submitting to a journal, you are joining a conversation, which we all do all the time in "real life". Unfortunately, as academics we sometimes leave our common sense behind in academic writing. So, let's look first at how this works in real life.

Joining a conversation: caution and care

Imagine that you are standing on the fringe of a group of strangers who are involved in a heated and long-standing discussion. What do you do if you really want to join that discussion?

Most people would listen for a quite a while to become familiar with the most important participants and get a gist of what the conversation is about. Then they might cautiously introduce themselves and offer a modest contribution that connects with an argument that was made by one of the key players.

If that's accepted, they might venture to offer slightly more involved contribution, but always one that acknowledges other points of views. Once they are more familiar with the conversation and its players, they might gradually start making slightly more provocative and radical suggestions. After a while they find the group is no longer a group of strangers and they become one of the key players in the conversation themselves. This also means that they can take the conversation in a completely new direction.

Or jumping right in...

In contrast, some people might ignore these conventions and just jump in with their own contribution – which might be completely unrelated to the discussion – at the first possible opportunity.

In most cases the response of the group will be something like: Who are you? How do you dare interrupting us? What are you talking about anyway? Don't you realise this has nothing to do with our discussion? Or... don't you realise we have considered this a long time ago and there were conclusive arguments against this?

Oftentimes, the group will "close ranks" and exclude the outsider, ignoring any further input from her. Very rarely, the group will say: "*Yes, she does have a point.*" Usually, this only happens if some of the people in the group were having doubts about where the discussion was going anyway and are grateful for an "outsider" saying what they didn't dare to say.

Journals: communities & conversations

Just like any collective of people, academic journals are communities. As communities, they revolve around academic conversations. These conversations might well be heated, as much as one can call academic discussions heated, and long-standing.

Unfortunately, many academics seem to forget their common sense when submitting to a journal. A large proportion of the submissions that journals receive seem to be of the following type:

> *Hello, you have never heard of me before, but please listen to this exciting, completely unrelated, thing I want to tell you. I haven't bothered to listen to anything that any of you said before, but I presume you are dying to hear what I have to say anyway.*

Academics are regularly submitting papers to journals dealing with a topic that has never featured in the journal before. Even worse, they make absolutely no attempt to explain why that topic might be relevant to the readers of that journal.

These days, most journal editors deal with this with a "desk reject", i.e., a rejection without the paper being sent out for review. Often, this leaves the author convinced that editors are biased against their research. Although no doubt this is sometimes true, most often it is not. Editors just feel that you are "barging into the conversation" without recognising the long tradition of scholarship in the field.

What to do? Research, research, research

Before submitting to a journal, you need to know what conversations are going on in the journal. Here is what you can do. First, make sure you use the free Publish or Perish software to find out which journals publish on your topic (see Chapter 4).

Then choose a few journals and research them carefully. At any step you can decide the journal is not a good fit and move on to the next journal:

1. Find the journal's mission statement and author guidelines and read them carefully.
2. Find out whether any of your colleagues have published in this journal. You can do this by searching by journal in your university repository. Ask for their advice, but be aware that a single

person's experience might not be typical. So, ideally triangulate by asking a couple of colleagues.

3. Talk to any senior colleagues who have published in a lot of different journals. Getting "a feel" for a journal's conversation comes with experience. Oftentimes a senior colleague can tell you instantly that "this is not a ... paper, you are much better off submitting to ..."

4. Find out whether the journal in question has published more specific guidance. Many journals publish "From the editors..." or "Publishing in..." type of articles that explain in detail what is expected of submissions. Searching the journal with the words editor OR editors in the **Title words** field should give you a pretty good overview. The screenshot below shows how you can do this – in seconds – in Publish or Perish.

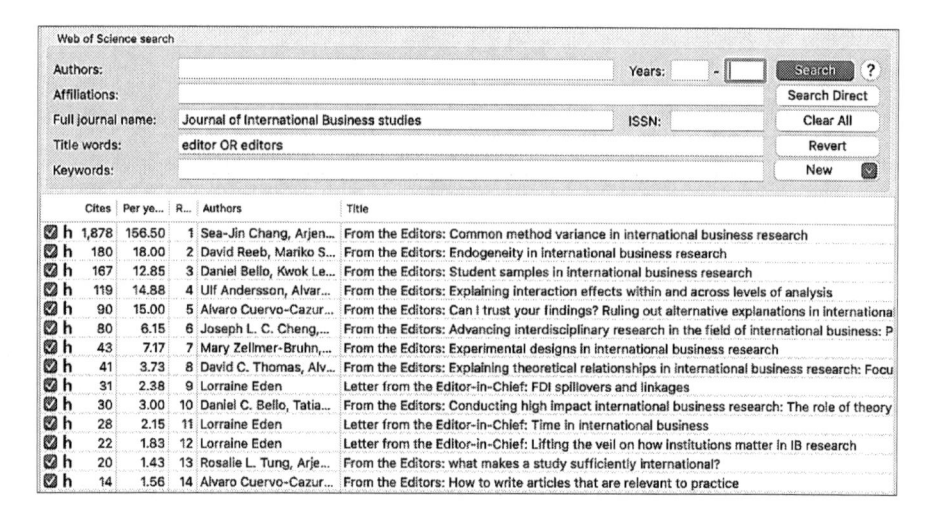

	Cites	Per ye...	R...	Authors	Title
☑ h	1,878	156.50	1	Sea-Jin Chang, Arjen...	From the Editors: Common method variance in international business research
☑ h	180	18.00	2	David Reeb, Mariko S...	From the Editors: Endogeneity in international business research
☑ h	167	12.85	3	Daniel Bello, Kwok Le...	From the Editors: Student samples in international business research
☑ h	119	14.88	4	Ulf Andersson, Alvar...	From the Editors: Explaining interaction effects within and across levels of analysis
☑ h	90	15.00	5	Alvaro Cuervo-Cazur...	From the Editors: Can I trust your findings? Ruling out alternative explanations in international
☑ h	80	6.15	6	Joseph L. C. Cheng,...	From the Editors: Advancing interdisciplinary research in the field of international business: P
☑ h	43	7.17	7	Mary Zellmer-Bruhn,...	From the Editors: Experimental designs in international business research
☑ h	41	3.73	8	David C. Thomas, Alv...	From the Editors: Explaining theoretical relationships in international business research: Focu
☑ h	31	2.38	9	Lorraine Eden	Letter from the Editor-in-Chief: FDI spillovers and linkages
☑ h	30	3.00	10	Daniel C. Bello, Tatia...	From the Editors: Conducting high impact international business research: The role of theory
☑ h	28	2.15	11	Lorraine Eden	Letter from the Editor-in-Chief: Time in international business
☑ h	22	1.83	12	Lorraine Eden	Letter from the Editor-in-Chief: Lifting the veil on how institutions matter in IB research
☑ h	20	1.43	13	Rosalie L. Tung, Arje...	From the Editors: what makes a study sufficiently international?
☑ h	14	1.56	14	Alvaro Cuervo-Cazur...	From the Editors: How to write articles that are relevant to practice

5. Find three *representative* and *recent* articles in this journal, preferably dealing with a topic related to your paper. Use these as model articles for the rest of your article preparation process, which will be described in Chapters 7-12.

Submit to only *one* journal at a time

PhD students and early career academics sometimes ask me if they can "speed up" the process through submitting their article to several journals at the same time and proceed with the journal that provides the quickest or best response. Please realise this would violate one of the (many) unwritten rules of academia and is something you should never do.

Submitting your article to more than one journal at the same time is a bit like being engaged to more than one person at the same time. There might be communities where this is acceptable, but by and large it is seriously frowned upon.

I know it is terribly frustrating to have to wait months for a decision and then (if rejected) start the whole process again. But remember, both the journal editor and reviewers are putting in a lot of time to review your paper and generally don't get any financial rewards for doing so. In the case of reviewers, there isn't even a reputational reward as the work is usually done without any public recognition.

Therefore, submitting to two journals at the same time is seen as unethical. It means that you are using (and even abusing) very scarce resources purely to your own advantage.

Don't ever think nobody will find out, academia is a very small world. The same person might be asked to review your paper for *both* journals, and they are not going to be pleased about that. Most likely they will inform the editors and both editors will reject your paper there and then.

And imagine what happens if you are not found out during the first round of the review process and both journals accept the article or give you a revise and resubmit. This means you will have to tell one of them: thanks, but no thanks! Do you think that this editor will ever look at another paper of yours again?

Publishing your work:
Engagement, dating or marriage?

The same proviso doesn't apply to "dating". Until the relationship gets more serious, most cultures will be fine with people dating more than one person at the same time.

The academic equivalent of this is presenting your paper at different university seminars and/or circulating it to informal reviewers. Academics do not expect "exclusivity" at that stage, although if you ask two or three of your senior colleagues for feedback it is "good form" to tell them others are also looking at it. Their time is valuable too.

Whether the same is true for submission to conferences is a bit of a grey area. You would certainly not be expected to submit the exact same paper to half a dozen conferences. Submitting a paper to two conferences is usually condoned, although it is not always officially sanctioned. You could well make a case for doing this for instance if the expected audience at the two conferences is quite different.

Duplicate publication in two different journals is a definite no-no. It is a bit like being married to two people at the same time. Of course, articles are sometimes reprinted in other languages, or in edited book collections. But this process always involves open and transparent negotiation, as well as copyright payments (the analogy with marriages obviously stops here!).

And yes, once an article is published, you are usually allowed to "publish" a pre-publication version of your paper on other fora, such as ResearchGate, Academia.edu, your university repository or your own academic website.

How to write for US journals with non-US data?

Another issue that often comes up in discussions with early career academics is whether there is any use in submitting to US journals if your research was conducted in another country. Academics often complain that US journals are biased against non-US data, making it hard for non-US academics to publish in these journals. Whilst there might well be a grain of truth to this, in this editorial Carol Kulik – a US academic who has been working in Australia since 2002 – argues that there might be another side to this story too.

- Kulik, C. T. (2005). **On editing in an international context**. *Journal of Management*, 31(2), 162-166.

She argues that every author tends to write for themselves. This is not a problem if the author is like the average reader of the journal. However, if they are psychologically or geographically different from the reader, this might create a bit of a problem. Rather than just seeing this as a problem, Kulik (Kulik, 2005:163) provides excellent suggestions on the need to make a particular country's context explicit for readers from another country.

> I would like to see all authors (non-U.S. and U.S.) explain why their questions are (or should be) of interest outside their country-of-origin. But even better, I would like to see authors go beyond this and highlight the unique strengths and benefits associated with their particular context.

> Non-U.S. authors sometimes try to bury the data's country of origin in the Methods section. If your assumption is that there is a bias against non-U.S. research, this may seem to be a sensible strategy. But reviewers hate this — it is the academic version of hiding in a closet and jumping out to yell "boo!" It sets off a string of sense-making questions in the mind of the reviewer ("Why didn't the author tell me earlier? Is there something problematic about this context?") that can cause exactly the opposite reviewer reaction than the author intended.

It is the author's responsibility to describe the context to the reviewer and help the reviewer to understand the broad theoretical questions that are being addressed within the context. As a rule, that means the context should be part of the material covered in the introduction.

How to avoid predatory journals?

Another key topic is how to avoid what are called predatory journals. They are called predatory because academics are "tricked" into publishing in them expecting them to be legitimate journals. They started to emerge in the early 2010s.

By that time academia was experiencing its very own type of spam: emails soliciting the respondent's submission to the journal in the email. The emails in question are invariably badly formatted and badly spelled, but they have one major draw card: the journals in question promise recipients that their article will be published very quickly. Oftentimes, they promise that the entire trajectory between submission and publication takes less than a month.

For many academics, especially PhD students or academics early in their career who are keen to publish their first article, this is quite an attractive prospect given that conventional academic journals – especially in the Social Sciences – can take from 1 to 5 years for this same process! There even seems to be a bit of competition going on to achieve the fastest turnaround time: one journal now even promises to provide peer review within a day and publication within 2 days after paying the processing fee.

The reason why these journals can promise such quick publication is of course that most of them do not actually engage in *any* sort of peer review. They will publish *any* article as long as authors are willing to pay the processing fee.

One creative author team even got a paper accepted that had the same sentence (Get me off your f------ mailing list) repeated for 10 pages, and illustrated with a flow diagram and a picture of the same request. The reviewer's report the authors received was just one word: "excellent".

Just like regular spammers, academic spammers are becoming smarter in their attempts at social engineering. Many now send out tailored emails that list a paper you have presented at a conference and express their interest in publishing it. An unsuspecting PhD student pressured to get a publication pipeline before going on the job market might be sorely tempted.

My recommendations

So, what is an inexperienced academic to do? Before submitting to a journal, I recommend you check:

- The editor's and editorial board's publication records

- Whether the journal's articles can be found in the Web of Science or Scopus (though see below) or at the very least in Google Scholar

- Some sample articles from the journal's website

As with any scam: "If it sounds too good to be true it usually is...."

Predatory journals: more than a fringe phenomenon

It would be easy to discard predatory journals as a fringe phenomenon, mainly targeted at unsuspecting authors in countries without strong scholarly traditions. However, some predatory open access journals managed to acquire a very central presence in the scholarly landscape.

By 2012, a Southeast Asian professor acquired all five top positions in Thomson Reuter's (now Clarivate) Essential Science Indicators' list of the 38 "Hot Papers" in their Business & Economics category. Moreover, Thomson Reuters awarded nine of the same Super-Author's publications, including his five "Hot Papers", their designation as "Highly Cited", i.e., being amongst the 1% most highly cited papers in the discipline for their year of publication.

Closer examination revealed that no less than 7 of his 9 most-highly-cited articles were published in one and the same journal, the Open Access journal *African Journal of Business & Management (AJBM)*. AJBM is one of many journals managed by Academic Journals, a commercial, Nigeria-based publisher. The remaining two articles were published in two other journals that were managed by the same publisher. Surprisingly, all three journals were listed in the Web of Science (they have since been removed).

AJBM published weekly issues and in 2011 published no less than 1350 articles. *It* also had a very high rate of within-journal citations; well over 90% of the articles citing this Super-Author's highly cited papers were from other articles published in the same journal. In fact, most citations were from the Super-Author himself. As this Super-Author published 41 Web of Science listed journal articles in just 2 years there was ample opportunity for self-citation.

Hence, even though these journals were ultimately removed from the Web of Science, this shows that listing in reputable data bases is not always a guarantee the journal is legitimate.

Predatory journals in Business & Management

With Nancy Adler I conducted a study of 45 predatory journals in Business & Management. My favourite part of our long journey of discovery was the mission statement for the *International Journal of Management*. Who wouldn't want to be a "budding genius" on their "platform for interactive pleasure and argumentative progression".

Transcending the familiar periphery of perfunctory substance, The International Journal of Management is offering to unfurl a newfangled panorama in the contemporary management study. We are rummaging around the web for progressive and clairvoyant minds for this exponential journal to focus upon various components of trade, marketing, finance, economy, and behavioral study.

This search can reach a culmination only with authors' as well as readers' cooperation at large. This is precisely meant to be an exploratory analysis over the given topics to stimulate the budding genius into aspiring eminent management personalities and present an international platform for interactive pleasure and argumentative progression. (http://www.theijm.com/, accessed January 2016)

Want to know more?

For a full write-up of the *AJBM* story, refer to my white paper: "How to become an author of ESI highly cited papers". The study about 45 predatory journals in Management that I referred to above was accepted in October 2014, but unfortunately did not escape the very publication delays it criticised, and was only published 1.5 years after being accepted.

- Harzing, A.W.; Adler N.J. (2016) **Disseminating knowledge: From potential to reality – New open-access journals collide with convention**, *Academy of Management Learning & Education*, vol. 15(1):140-156.

Conclusion

In this chapter we focused on targeting the right journal. I explained why it is crucial to understand that academic journals are communities engaged in conversations and how to ensure you are selecting the right conversation to contribute to. We also shed some light on three key questions: concurrent submission, writing for US journals with non-US data, and a relatively recent academic phenomenon: predatory journals.

The next eight chapters cover a structured approach to ensuring your paper gets past the first hurdle in the peer review process, the desk-reject (Chapter 6) focusing on Titles (Chapter 7), Abstracts (Chapter 8), Introductions (Chapter 9), Conclusions (Chapter 10), Using references strategically (Chapter 11), Writing a letter to the Editor (Chapter 12), and other things you can do to improve your chances (Chapter 13).

Chapter 6: How to avoid a desk-reject?

A desk-reject indicates that your manuscript has been rejected by a journal without it being sent out for review. This means that you need to try your luck at another journal. But even worse, you also receive preciously little advice how to improve your chances.

Although some journals – especially those that have (a) separate desk-reject editor(s) – provide you with substantive feedback on rejection, most desk-rejects are accompanied by only a few lines, mainly communicating that the paper "doesn't fit" the journal.

So, for many academics a desk-reject causes extreme disappointment, a feeling that can easily turn into desperation if the same outcome is repeated over and over again with different journals.

"How to avoid a desk-reject" is therefore the theme of the yearly writing bootcamp that I am running at Middlesex University as part of our efforts to create an inclusive, supportive, and collaborative research culture. At the bootcamp we work with a structured 7-step process; I will discuss each of these seven steps in turn in the seven upcoming chapters. But first, a bit of context...

Why are desk-rejects increasing?

The number of desk-rejects has increased very rapidly in the last two decades. Whereas in the past only completely hopeless papers would suffer this fate, these days desk-reject rates for top journals can be as high as 50-80%. The reason for this is simple arithmetic: the number of journal submissions has also increased dramatically.

For example, even the top journals in Management would only get a few hundred submissions a year in the past, of which they might publish 30 to 40. Nowadays many of these journals receive well over 1,000 submissions a year. Some journals have expanded their issues and thus the number of published articles, but most still only publish around 50-100 articles a year.

This means that if they didn't use desk-rejects, editors would need to find reviewers for well over 1,000 papers a year, 90-95% of which would not make it through the review process. With every paper needing 2 or 3 reviewers, that would mean finding a few thousand reviewers every year.

Moreover, most academics do not accept all review requests they are receiving. So, it is not unusual for an editor to have to contact 4 or 5 academics to find a single reviewer. So, without using desk-rejects an editor might well need to contact 10,000-15,000 academics a year. And that's just for a single journal! This is clearly not a feasible proposition.

Even worse, academics might agree to review a manuscript for a journal, but then discover that the paper is of very poor quality. This might mean that writing the desired "constructive" review takes one or two full days to the task rather than a few hours. As a result, they are unlikely to accept the next review request from the same journal, or in fact any journal! Hence, editors need to be very careful with their "reviewer resources" and will generally only send out papers for review if there is a reasonable chance that they might get a revise & resubmit.

Most editors can easily identify the bottom 40-60% of the submissions; it is also relatively easy for them to pick the top 1-5%, those papers that have a high likelihood of successfully getting through the review process. The difficulty lies in the middle group, the "not sure, might have a chance if...". Quality differences in this category are generally small, but the editor needs to make a binary decision yes/no decision.

My aim with this 7-step process is to increase your chances that this decision falls into the "yes, send out for review" category rather than into the "no, it's a desk-reject" category. So, rather than focusing on the longer-term goal of getting your paper published, the first intermediate goal should be to get your paper into the review process. Even if you don't manage to get a revise & resubmit after the first round of reviews, at least you will get some feedback from experts in your field.

Moreover, even if you are submitting to journals that do not (yet) have a high proportion of desk-rejects, following this 7-step process will make it much easier to get through the review process without hiccups. It is also likely to result in a much better paper.

Are you ready? Ten practical signs

Before we move on to the 7 steps in the next seven chapters, here are ten practical signs that indicate you are not quite ready to join the conversation of a particular journal:

1. You have picked the journal in question because it is a highly ranked journal, but it is a not journal that you normally read.

2. Your references do not include a single reference to the journal in question. Obviously, you should not just cite *any* paper in the journal to get into the editor's good books. However, if you cannot find any reason to cite a single paper from the journal, maybe this means there is no "conversation" about your topic.

3. [a variant on point #2] You think there are very good reasons for not having any references to the journal you submit to, but you do not have any references to any *other* journals in the same sub-discipline either. I recently had to review a paper that was submitted to *Journal of International Business Studies* which didn't have *any* references to *any* articles in *any* International Business journal.

4. [a variant on point #2] You can make matters even worse by submitting to a journal and not having any references to any

53

journals in the entire discipline. The paper I referred to under #3 didn't include *any* references to *any* journals in Business & Management. Of course, we all do believe in interdisciplinary work, but it is up to you as an author to make the *connection* between the disciplines.

5. Your formatting and referencing style do not conform to the journal style. Yes, I know it is frustrating to have to reformat your paper every time you submit to a new journal. But most editors will reason that if you can't be bothered to do a little reformatting, they can't be bothered to consider your paper seriously.

6. You use British spelling when submitting to a US journal or vice-versa.

7. The structure of your paper is completely different to the structure of most of the papers published in the journal. For instance, you do not have a section on practical implications in a journal that prides itself on being a "bridge" journal.

8. You submit a review paper, theoretical paper, meta-analysis, empirical paper, literature review, or experimental paper to a journal that has never published any of these types of papers before, or has a mission to publish only one type of paper.

9. A Publish or Perish search for the journal with your keywords in the **Title words** box doesn't provide a single result.

10. Your paper contains many claims saying that you are the *"first academic ever"* to study or do something. Although this might well be true in *some* cases, in most cases it simply signals you haven't done a proper literature review. In fact, this means you are probably not ready to submit to *any* journal yet ☺.

Conclusion

This chapter explained the phenomenon of desk-rejects. The next seven chapters cover a structured approach to ensuring your paper gets past this first hurdle in the peer review process, focusing on Titles (Chapter 7), Abstracts (Chapter 8), Introductions (Chapter 9), Conclusions (Chapter 10), Using references strategically (Chapter 11), Writing a letter to the Editor (Chapter 12), and other things you can do to improving your chances (Chapter 13).

Chapter 7: Your title: The public face of your paper

Your manuscript's title is the first thing an editor sees. So, make sure it grabs their attention and clearly communicates what the paper is about. Creating a good title is an iterative process. This chapter therefore provides some tips of what to include in the title and how to improve on your first attempt. I will also give you some examples of "Title transformations" from the yearly writing bootcamp that I run at Middlesex University.

A good title is descriptive...

Obviously, a title needs to be descriptive, not just for the editor, but also for future readers. They need to be able to find it when they search for articles on the topic. This means that ideally you would include the following:

1. The main concepts and/or research question

2. The country or industry context or the population studied if it is unusual

3. The research method if it is unusual

Some academics are tempted to omit the second and third points from their title as they think it might disadvantage their paper if it is not a mainstream country, industry, population, or research method. However, the editor and reviewers don't like surprises. Omitting this information might well lead to a more negative assessment. It is better to set their expectations from the start.

... or quirky? Try both!

Although descriptive is safe, a slightly unusual title that is combined with a descriptive sub-title might attract interest and make the paper more memorable to its readers. This might matter more *after* publication, but could still help to make the paper stand out in the review process. Below I provide some examples of how this might work.

My former PhD student Shea Fan studied the role of ethnic identity in the relationship between local employees in a multinational and ethnically similar expatriates. Quite a few of her article titles used a main title that referred to this phenomenon in an abstract sense through alliteration (*The Benefits of Being Understood...*) or wordplay (*How you see me, how you don't...*), making them more memorable.

A paper that reviewed the role of language differences in HQ-subsidiary communication used a multi-lingual main title (*Hablas vielleicht un peu la mia language ...*) – including words in Spanish, German, French, Italian and English –to convey the article's key challenge. Be warned though that this might be a risky strategy. One of the paper's reviewers commented: "*there has been a mistake in the title as part of it is not in English*". S/he clearly didn't quite get the point...

In an article on the role of expatriates in controlling subsidiaries, I used an animal analogy (*Of bears, bumblebees, and spiders...*) to reflect direct personal control (an over**bear**ing bear), socialization (bumblebees spreading corporate culture through cross-pollination), and informal communication (spiders weaving communication webs).

This made the article stick in people's minds; quite a few academics that met me for the first time said: "*Oh, you are the lady of the bears, bumble-bees and spiders*". It inspired one of my co-authors, Ling Zhang, to use a similar analogy in a paper on cultural identity negotiation: *Of ostriches, frogs, birds, and lizards.*

How to improve your title?

Once you have a draft title, get a few colleagues together and ask for their opinion. Do they understand what the paper is about? You will find that working with academics from different backgrounds really helps you to sharpen the focus of your title. This will make it more attractive to a broader audience. Return the favour for their paper; this really shouldn't take more than 10-15 minutes per paper.

Below are two examples by my Middlesex colleagues Parisa Dashtipour and Athina Dilmperi. They both managed to get past the desk-reject stage for their chosen top journal and after several rounds of revisions got their papers published in their preferred journal. Of course, this wasn't solely due to their changed title, but every little bit helps.

- **OLD:** Social defences in occupational identity construction: A focus group study of nurses in training
- Issues with the old title
  - Doesn't mention the core concept of the article (compassion)
  - Doesn't mention the approach (psychosocial)
  - Rather too many nouns linked by prepositions
- **NEW:** 'Compassion' as social defence: A psychosocial focus group study of trainee nurses' identity construction
  - More active/agentic: "as social defence" instead of "social defences in"
  - Clearer that this is about nurses' identity

Title transformations

- **OLD**: The Role of Cultural Brand Assets in Destination Branding
- Issues with the old title
  - There are (too) many articles on destination branding already
  - No reference to the unique contribution, i.e., city branding
  - No indication that the study looks at more than one destination
- **NEW**: What makes a City Unique? Cultural City Assets in Three Cultural Destinations

Title transformations

Some quick fine-tuning tips

- Search for your title in Google Scholar. If you get too many similar results, you might want to make it more unique.

- If your title includes both your independent and dependent variables, clearly indicate which is which. This might be clear to you, but it unlikely to be clear to every reader.

- Here is a list of some frequently used sleep-inducing empty waffle words that are better avoided. Instead, you could use "Between [...] and [...]". This also clearly indicates a relationship between two concepts and is much punchier:
    - examining the relationship between ...,
    - the effect of ...,
    - the influence of ...

- towards a framework of …,
- a comparison of …

- Avoid using "towards a..." altogether. This suggests you are "not quite there yet", which obviously reduces the perceived contribution of your paper.

Chapter 8: Writing your abstract: Not a last-minute activity

Recognise this scenario? You have finally finished your paper and realise that you have forgotten to write the abstract. You cobble one together from sentences in the paper and try to submit your paper online. It turns out the journal has a strict word limit for the abstract and the system won't let you go through. So, you quickly cut a few words or sentences and press submit. The paper comes back within a week with a desk-reject. One thing the editor mentions is that the abstract doesn't clearly communicate the paper's contribution.

The abstract might well be *the* most important part of your paper, both in the review process and once the paper is published. So, it is crucial to get the abstract right. With the title it creates the paper's first impression. With the introduction and conclusion, it might be the only part of the paper that overworked editors read before they decide on a desk-reject.

So, writing your abstract is not a last-minute activity and requires a lot of trial and error! This chapter provides you with some tips on what to include in your abstract and how to improve on your first draft.

What needs to be included in an abstract?

As with any part of a manuscript, the exact format of the abstract can be very discipline and journal specific. However, in my own discipline – Management – an abstract generally needs to include:

- Research background, sets the scene and explains why the topic is important (in real life, not just to academics).

- Research gap, what it is that we do not yet know about this topic?

- Research topic/question, what exactly is your paper about?

- Theory you draw on (if any).

- Research methods and data that are used in the paper.

- Key results: ensure that you include the actual *content* of your results, not something like *"we present our results which confirm/conflict with prior research"*, which doesn't tell the reader anything.

- Implications for theory & practice, this part can sometimes be left out in a 100-word abstract. If you do include this, don't write *"we discuss implications for theory and practice"*, but tell the reader *what* they are.

Most journals only allow 100-200 words for an abstract and will not let you submit your manuscript if the abstract is even *one* word over the wordcount. Including all the above information within this wordcount is challenging, so often you will need to find a way to creatively combine the many different elements in one sentence.

In the next section, I have provided two examples to illustrate this. For more examples, please download the slides accompanying my writing bootcamp (see also my blogpost *"Middlesex 2022 ECR event: back to Cumberland Lodge"*) or watch the relevant video *"Publishing in top journals – Bonus session"* on my YouTube Channel, called Harzing Academic Resources.

Two example abstracts

Both papers were published in the *Journal of World Business*, which has a strict 100-word limit for its abstracts. So, every single word counts. You will see that both abstracts cover most components that were discussed above. However, they are very different, reflecting the different emphasis of the two papers.

Introducing a new concept to the field

In this article, one of my former PhD students, Shea Fan, introduced the psychological concept of (ethnic) identity confirmation to the field of International Business, with a special focus on ethnically similar expatriates.

As this was a very new concept, it was essential to define it in the abstract. This ensured reviewers read the paper in the right frame of mind. However, this took up a lot of words which meant that other elements of the abstract had to be curtailed or omitted.

- **Background:** Employing expatriates who share an ethnicity with host country employees (HCEs) is a widespread expatriate selection strategy.
- **Research gap:** However, little research has compared how expatriates and HCEs perceive this shared ethnicity.
- **Research topic:** Drawing upon an identity perspective, we propose HCEs' ethnic identity confirmation, *the level of agreement between how an HCE views the importance of his/her own ethnic identity and how expatriates view the importance of the HCE's ethnic identity*, affects HCEs' attitudes towards ethnically similar expatriates.
- **Research method and results:** Results of two experiments show that HCEs' ethnic identity confirmation is related to HCEs' perception of expatriates' trustworthiness and knowledge-sharing intention.

Example abstract: new concept

Fan, S.X.; Harzing, A.W. (2017) Host country employees' ethnic identity confirmation: Evidence from interactions with ethnically similar expatriates, Journal of World Business, vol. 52, no. 5, 640-652.

Providing empirical rigour to existing concepts

Research into language differences in multinational companies had been largely based on interview data, covering only a limited number of home and host countries. This makes it difficult to assess to what extent these results are generalisable to other countries.

This article – the fourth and last of my articles on language barriers in MNCs – therefore reported on a large-scale scale quantitative study. This study, which was conducted with subsidiaries in more than 13 host countries, with their headquarters located in more than 25 different countries, showed that language policies and practices were very different across different home and host country contexts.

This article was thus mainly data-driven and descriptive, rather than theory-driven and analytical. Therefore, the focus in the abstract is on the method and results, as well as the implications for management, instead of on the research gap/topic and theory.

> - **Background:** The importance of language differences in multinational companies (MNCs) can hardly be overlooked.
> - **Research gap/topic:** This article therefore provides the <u>first large-scale quantitative overview</u> of language competencies, policies and practices in MNCs.
> - **Method:** It is based on <u>data from more than 800 subsidiaries, located in thirteen different countries with headquarters in more than 25 different countries</u>, which were aggregated into four distinct home country clusters.
> - **Results:** This comprehensive study allows us to differentiate prior conceptual or case-based findings according to home, host and corporate languages…
> - **Implications for management:** …and to develop managerial implications which vary according to the different country clusters.
>
> **Example abstract: data emphasis**
>
> Harzing, A.W.; Pudelko, M. (2013) Language competencies, policies and practices in multinational corporations: A comprehensive review and comparison of Anglophone, Asian, Continental European and Nordic MNCs, Journal of World Business, vol. 48, no. 1, pp. 87-97.

Some quick fine-tuning tips

- Find highly cited papers in your field and look at the abstract for ideas for good practice
- Make a list of keywords and ensure they are either in the title or the abstract. Keywords should include:

- key concepts + method,
- level of analysis,
- context if it is unusual, unique, or a key contribution

• Send your abstract to the gym!
    - Cut flabby fat [waffle words]
    - Tighten and tone up, ensure every word counts. Nearly every abstract can be improved by cutting words. Cutting words makes you focus on the essentials
    - Many of us clutter our writing with qualifiers and irrelevant digressions; although this can be tolerated in the main text, it is often fatal in the abstract

• Some specifics
    - Don't use abbreviations in your abstract
    - Most journals don't like references in abstracts
    - Some good words to highlight your unique contribution: reframe, reinterpret, reformulate, bridges, shift in focus, profound implications

Chapter 9: Your introduction: First impressions count!

After the abstract, the introduction might be the most important part of your paper. It is the part of the paper where you need to tell the editor and the reader *directly and clearly* why they need to read the paper.

With the title and abstract, it also creates the paper's first impression and sets the tone for the rest of the article. In combination with the conclusion, these might be the only parts of the paper that overworked editors read before deciding on a desk-reject. It is therefore not unusual to spend a third of your writing time on perfecting these sections and write half a dozen versions.

This chapter provides you with tips on what to include in a good introduction and how to ensure the title, abstract and introduction work in harmony, each building on the other.

Emails vs. paper introductions

Paper introductions are a lot like emails. Imagine reading an email like this: *"Blah Blah Blah Blah and oh... by the way I want you to do this."*. You wouldn't be likely to comply, would you? Yet this is what many paper introductions read like. If you write to someone you haven't emailed for a while or at all, you are likely to include:

- a bit of context, such as how do you know the person or where you last met them,
- what the email is about and why it is important,
- why it is in their interest to respond to the email [what is in it for them].

An introduction to an academic paper is not that different, you provide context, explain why your research topic is important, and tell the reader what is in it for them.

Provide the context

You don't jump straight into your research topic. First you need to establish the context of an area you research by:

- Highlighting the importance of the topic (in *real* life), and/or
- Making general statements about the topic, and/or
- Presenting a brief overview on current research on the subject.

Argue for your topic's importance

Next, you identify your research niche by:

- Opposing an existing assumption, and/or
- Revealing not only a gap in the existing research, but crucially also explaining why this gap is important, and/or
- Studying the topic in a new context and explaining why this context is important.

Remember, just because something hasn't been studied before, doesn't mean it *needs* to be studied. You need to answer the "so what" question. Why is this topic important?

As is humorously illustrated by Jon Billsberry, editor of the *Journal of Management Education*, belly button fluff build-up is one of a million topics that hasn't been studied (see slide), but does that mean it should be? More seriously, just because there is a gap in the literature that doesn't mean it *needs* to be filled.

Seeing research as gap-filling might lead to what is called Polyfilla research. Science is cumulative, so any of our research articles might only add one little brick to the house of knowledge. As academics we are not expected to add an entire wall, let alone design a new house. However, you *do* need to ensure that you are not just filling a hairline crack.

> **BELLY BUTTONS**
>
> Billsberry, J. (2013). A longitudinal empirical study into the buildup of fluff in my belly button. *Journal of Management Education*, 37(5), 595-600.
>
> "I conducted this study because there was a gap in the literature."
>
> **The most common mistake: polyfilla research**
>
> Source: John Billsberry presentation at Middlesex University, 5 March 2018

The other thing that we need to keep in mind is the mortar between the gaps. In Chapter 5 we talked about how submitting an article to a journal should be seen as joining a scholarly conversation. If you want to join a conversation by adding another brick of knowledge, you do need to first acknowledge the other bricks that are already there.

But you also need to connect your new brick of knowledge in some way to the other bricks. That's where the mortar comes in. Without mortar your brick will not "adhere", without proper connections your new brick of knowledge will not be joined with the other bricks of knowledge. So, think very carefully about how you can connect the new knowledge that you are adding in your article to the existing knowledge.

> **You are adding a "new brick of knowledge"**
>
> **You are not "filling a gap" [hairline crack]**
>
> **You are not building an entire new house, but...**

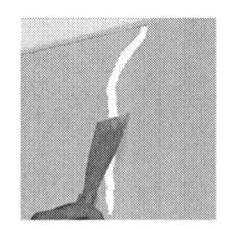

Here is an extended example of how to do this based on one of my recent papers (you can read more about this paper in this blogpost: *"Beyond expatriation: How inpatriation supports subsidiary growth and performance"*).

INTRODUCTION

Intra-company knowledge transfer has long been acknowledged as a key source of competitive advantage for multinational companies (MNCs) (Bartlett & Ghoshal, 1989; Gupta & Govindarajan, 2000; Kogut & Zander, 1993), and this knowledge is usually embedded in individuals (Argote, 1999; Nonaka, 1994). Thus, 'mobility of individuals' is a powerful mechanism for facilitating knowledge transfer in MNCs. Traditionally, expatriation has featured prominently in this discussion (Caligiuri & Bonache, 2016; Harzing, 2001). More recently, as scholars have turned their attention to the diversification of global work arrangements (Collings, 2014; Collings & Isichei, 2017; Reiche, Lee, & Allen, 2019), inpatriation has received increasing attention (e.g., Duvivier, Peeters, & Harzing, 2019; Harzing, Pudelko, & Reiche, 2016). An inpatriate is defined as an employee who is transferred from an MNC subsidiary to the corporation's headquarters (HQ) for a limited period of time (Harvey & Buckley, 1997). After Reiche (2006, 2011) first demonstrated inpatriates' role in knowledge transfer, recent research has provided some evidence that inpatriation is a complementary or possibly even superior means of knowledge transfer between subsidiaries and HQ (Duvivier et al., 2019; Harzing et al., 2016). However, we know little about the *process* and strategic *outcomes* of inpatriates' knowledge transfer after returning from their assignment at HQ.

What's in it for the reader?

Finally, you place your own research within the important research niche that you have outlined by doing four things in the next four paragraphs: stating the intent of your study, outlining its key characteristics, describing important study results and contributions, and giving a brief overview of the paper. For each of these I have included an example of the same paper that I used above.

Stating the intent of your study

Here you explain what it is *exactly* that you are aiming to do in your study. This should include a clear research question. Again though, make sure that you don't just state the intent of *your* study, but also carefully connect it to prior research in the field.

> Our central research question therefore explores whether and how inpatriates' knowledge transfer activities provide value to their subsidiary. Drawing on insights from organizational knowledge creation theory (Nonaka, 1994), our study investigates how inpatriates transfer knowledge and contribute to subsidiary capability building and subsidiary evolution (Birkinshaw & Hood, 1998; Gupta & Govindarajan, 2000; Luo, 2002). We define subsidiary capability building as developing a subsidiary's distinctive resources and unique skills through learning from other organizations (in this case HQ) and creating new business opportunities. In turn, subsidiary evolution is the consequence of a subsidiary's accumulated capabilities, resulting in a change in the roles and responsibilities of a subsidiary in the differentiated MNC network (Birkinshaw & Hood, 1998; Luo, 2002). By linking inpatriates' knowledge transfer to these two performance-related outcomes, we respond to calls for more empirical work that substantiates inpatriation as a source of strategic value to MNCs (Moeller & Reiche, 2017).

Outlining the key characteristics of your study

Here you explain the methods you have used to collect your data (assuming it is an empirical paper). It is important to not just outline your methods, but also explain why these methods are the ones that are best suited for your study. This is also the place to explain the context in which your study was conducted.

> To generate rich data and insights we opted for a qualitative research strategy (Patton, 2002). Our case study approach is an especially suitable method as it enables unique insights into how certain conditions change over time and move towards a certain outcome (Pettigrew, 1990; Soulsby & Clark, 2011). Further, to extend the geographical base of inpatriation research beyond its traditional focus on Western countries (for reviews see Moeller & Reiche, 2017; Moeller & Harvey, 2018), we chose Japanese MNCs operating in Asia as our research context in line with recent empirical studies in the Asian region (e.g., Sarabi, Froese & Hamori, 2017). Our data, derived from 40 interviews in Japanese MNCs' HQs and their overseas subsidiaries as well as three forms of time-stamped archival data, illuminate the short- and long-term functions of inpatriation that contribute to subsidiary capability building and subsidiary evolution.

Describing important results and contributions

In the next part of the introduction, you describe the most important results of your study, again taking care to explain exactly how they contribute to current research in the area.

> In line with recent calls for further research into the strategic value of international human resource management (IHRM) more broadly (e.g., Andersson, Brewster, Minbaeva, Narula, & Wood, 2019; McNulty & Brewster, 2017), our study bridges and contributes to both the IHRM and the global strategy literatures. Our findings disentangle the explanatory mechanisms through which short-term functions of inpatriation (the acquisition of task knowledge, language/cultural knowledge, and relational knowledge) develop into long-term functions (building subsidiary absorptive capability, and maintaining access to information), which in turn result in subsidiary capability building and subsidiary evolution. In doing so, we derive a theoretical model that highlights why successive and long-term inpatriation is critical in this process.
>   We advance research in three distinct areas that emphasize different stages of this model. First, our empirical evidence shows how the individual tacit knowledge that inpatriates acquired at HQ is converted into organizational knowledge upon their return to their original subsidiaries. Specifically, we demonstrate how organizational knowledge creation theory (Nonaka, 1994) can be expanded to the MNC context, and how this theory could serve as a fruitful lens to further investigate the dynamic link between IHRM and the performance-related outcomes of knowledge transfer. Second, we extend existing work on inpatriates' knowledge transfer role (Reiche, 2011; Duvivier et al., 2019; Harzing et al., 2016) by identifying how inpatriates' knowledge transfer provides strategic *value* to subsidiaries in the form of the performance-related outcomes of subsidiary capabilities and subsidiary evolution. Third, our study contributes to the global strategy literature by suggesting that the successive use of inpatriation serves as an effective process for subsidiary evolution. In particular, we provide a deeper understanding of how a subsidiary, as a result of an increasing number of returning inpatriates over time, transforms itself from a passive recipient of HQ knowledge to an active contributor to the MNC network. This is in line with global strategy scholars' recent focus on examining the micro-foundations of firm-level concepts, including knowledge transfer (Contractor, Foss, Kundu, & Lahiri, 2019; Foss & Pedersen, 2019; Tippmann, Scott, & Mangematin, 2014).

As you can see in the two paragraphs above, we first provided a summary of our key findings. Then in the second paragraph, we started by explaining how our study contributes to organizational knowledge creation theory. Subsequently, we demonstrated how it advances our knowledge on the role of inpatriates as agents of knowledge transfer, thereby contributing to the international HRM literature. Finally, we showed how our paper contributes to the Global Strategy literature by connecting global mobility to the topic of subsidiary evolution.

Giving a brief overview of the structure of the paper

Finally, it is customary to provide a brief overview of the structure of your paper, though in some journals this might be seen as superfluous. Refer to examples from the journal you are targeting to see whether this is required.

> The remainder of this article is structured as follows. First, we review the literature on organizational knowledge creation, inpatriates' knowledge transfer, subsidiary capability building and subsidiary evolution. Then, we provide a detailed account of our qualitative research design, the three phases of data collection, and the data analysis based on our 'temporal bracketing strategy'. Subsequently, we present the findings through which we build our theoretical model. We conclude with the theoretical and managerial implications of our study and suggest three directions for further research.

How title, abstract and introduction work in harmony

These three elements of your manuscript should build on each other, with each of them providing gradually more detail on your study. So, once you have written a first draft review them as a package and make sure they work in complete harmony.

Title

The title includes the key concepts and research question (or sometimes the key conclusion). The title of the study that I discussed above was *"How does successive inpatriation contribute to subsidiary capability building and subsidiary evolution? An organizational knowledge creation perspective."*

This includes the study's key concepts (successive inpatriation, subsidiary capability building, and subsidiary evolution) in a sentence highlighting the research question, but also – implicitly – the theory we are contributing to (organizational knowledge creation).

Abstract

The abstract unpacks each of these key concepts and the research question, but also includes a background/context, methods, results, and implications. Here is the abstract of the study I discussed above.

ABSTRACT

Intra-company knowledge transfer is a key source of competitive advantage for multinational companies (MNCs) and this knowledge is usually embedded in individuals. Drawing on organizational knowledge creation theory, we explore how inpatriation contributes to knowledge transfer and, in turn, subsidiary performance. Inpatriation involves the international assignment of employees from an MNC's foreign subsidiary to its headquarters. Despite increasing attention to the role of inpatriation, we lack a clear understanding of whether and how inpatriates provide value to their subsidiaries after returning from headquarters. Through a qualitative case study of Japanese MNCs, we demonstrate the process through which inpatriates' knowledge transfer contributes to subsidiary capability building and subsidiary evolution over time and explain why successive inpatriation is thus critical to enhance subsidiary performance. Our theoretical model highlights the value of inpatriates as knowledge agents, reveals the process through which inpatriates transfer knowledge between HQ and subsidiaries, and provides a more nuanced understanding of the micro-foundations of intra-MNC knowledge transfer processes. Based on these findings, we argue that inpatriation is not merely a staffing method that is complementary to expatriation, but a key practice in its own right to support subsidiaries' growth and performance.

Introduction

Finally, the introduction is a complete mini version of the paper. The emphasis is on the study context, a brief literature review showing the importance of the research gap, the research question, and the study's key contributions. The methods, results and implications for theory and practice are only discussed briefly, if at all, as these have separate sections later on in the manuscript.

Chapter 10: Conclusions: Last impressions count too!

First impressions count! They also set anchoring effects. This notion applies to both real-life interactions and academic articles. That is why Titles (Chapter 7), Abstracts (Chapter 8), and Introductions (Chapter 9) are so important to avoid falling at the first hurdle of the peer review process.

But even so, last impressions are important too. At the end of any meeting, you normally recap the agreements you made, reinforce how nice it was to meet your counterpart, and maybe tell them what you enjoyed in particular. You do not usually end a meeting with a reminder of all the things you didn't agree about, or a social occasion with all the things that you disliked.

So, why do so many academics end their paper with limitations? Of course, you need to note your study's limitations, but do that as part of the discussion section, *not* the concluding section. Ending a paper with limitations – even when you pair them with suggestions for future research – will leave your reader disappointed. They might well ask themselves, why on earth did I bother to read this paper if there is so much wrong with it? So please: don't *don't* **don't** end your paper with limitations.

What *do* you include in conclusions?

Most academic journals have considerable flexibility in their expectations for concluding sections. However, in Management journals you would typically conclude your paper with a short paragraph which briefly summarizes the entire study.

The conclusion is the mirror image of the abstract and often includes the same elements that we have discussed there (research background/context, research gap, research question, methods, results, and they study's implications). Typically, it devotes a bit more attention to the wider implications of the paper than the abstract. It might also have a specific call for action at the end. Here are two examples.

Theory/concept focused conclusion

In this article, one of my former PhD students, Shea Fan, introduced the psychological concept of ethnic identity confirmation to the field of international business, with a special focus on ethnically similar expatriates. Shea also published an article based on dyadic survey data, a conceptual article, and a practitioner-oriented article based on interview data. This article, however, was the first to be published. It thus needed to introduce the concept to an audience unfamiliar with the theory. This is what we did in the Abstract (see Chapter 8).

- **Research background/gap:** To date, the expatriate literature has rarely focused on HCEs' experiences.
- **Research topic:** Based on the context of ethnically similar expatriate-HCE interactions, we have identified ethnic identity confirmation as a key factor that influences their relationships. We specifically focused on HCEs and investigated their ethnic identity confirmation.
- **Research method + high-level results:** Using both an experiment and a quasi-experimental method, we have demonstrated that HCEs' ethnic identity confirmation is an important facilitator influencing HCEs' attitudes towards expatriates.
- **Wider conceptual/theoretical implications:** This concept also captures an overlooked interpersonal dynamic - ethnic identity confirmation - among HCEs and expatriates who share the same ethnicity. It, thus, provides a promising new perspective in exploring interactions between expatriates and HCEs.

Example: theory focused conclusion

Fan, S.X.; Harzing, A.W. (2017) Host country employees' ethnic identity confirmation: Evidence from interactions with ethnically similar expatriates, Journal of World Business, vol. 52, no. 5, 640-652.

In the conclusion, we focused on the study's key contributions: the focus on host country employees rather than expatriates, and the use of experimental methods, something which was still very uncommon at the time in the field of international business. However, we ended the conclusion by emphasising the theoretical/conceptual contribution again, as – rather than the specific results – this is what we felt to be the study's core contribution.

Context/action focused conclusion

This article was one of a series in which we investigated the level of gender and international diversity in editorial boards of academic journals. We found that geographical diversity of editorial boards had increased over time, but that a very large proportion of board members still came from the home country, a tendency that was strongest in US journals which had more than 80% home country membership.

- **Context 1:** An increased emphasis on formal research evaluation means that academics in more and more countries are expected to publish in top journals.
- **Context 2:** Their ability to do so might be compromised by the fact that the largest proportion of the gatekeepers in these journals are part of a dominant group.
- **Research gap:** It is therefore important to understand the level of international diversity in editorial boards as well as the factors influencing this diversity.
- **High-level results:** Our study, the first large-scale investigation of this phenomenon, found that encouraging progress has been made in the area of international diversity.
- **Action needed:** However, continued active management by editors, professional associations and individual academics alike is necessary to ensure that our editorial boards properly reflect the diverse management community.

Example: Context/action focused conclusion

Harzing, A.W.; Metz, I. (2013) Practicing what we preach: The geographic diversity of editorial boards, Management International Review, vol. 53, no. 2, pp. 169-187.

Instead of focusing on the specific results in the concluding section, we decided to end the paper a strong call for action by focusing not only on the importance of diversity in editorial boards, but also on the possible consequences of a lack of diversity. We felt that this was necessary to ensure that the parties involved would take the required action to ensure that editorial boards reflect the diverse community of management scholars.

How to end your paper effectively?

What academics will remember from your paper is dependent on its final couple of sentences. So, always try to end the paper on a strong note by recapping its key contributions. Ensure that the last sentence or the last 2-3 short sentences of your paper can be read on their own. They need to provide readers with a powerful take-away. I haven't always followed my own advice, but here are some articles where I did.

> *We thus argue that a fair and inclusive cross-disciplinary comparison of research performance is possible, provided we use Google Scholar or Scopus as a data source, and the recently introduced hI, annual – a h-index corrected for career length and co-authorship patterns – as the metric of choice. [Harzing & Alakangas, 2016]*

> *In this article we have provided the first large-scale empirical analysis of the language barrier and its solutions. Our conclusions mirror Feely & Harzing's (2003:50) conceptual article in that it is important to "understand the language barrier well and to mix and match the solutions into a blend that is right for the company context". Most importantly though, MNCs should take the language barrier seriously. Only then will MNCs be able to progress in tackling the language barrier and increase their competitiveness on a global scale. [Harzing, Köster & Magner, 2011]*

Given the particular challenges of international survey research that we described above, many areas in the field of international management still remain largely under-researched, even though they provide ample opportunities to advance our knowledge. However, we hope that by identifying some of the key issues in international survey research and offering various solutions, we have been able to encourage and promote such future research. [Harzing, Reiche & Pudelko, 2013]

Consequently, we recommend that studies in International Business focus first and foremost on home and host country context and resist the temptation to use (cultural) distance as a catchall concept, thus avoiding an illusion of causality, which ultimately hinders the potential of International Business research to provide useful guidance to managers on key International Business phenomena. [Harzing & Pudelko, 2016]

Chapter 11: What do you cite? Using references strategically

You've polished your title, abstract, introduction and conclusion. Time to submit? Well, not quite. Before you do so, take a critical look at the references you use in your paper.

References fulfil many different functions in academic articles. For an overview, refer to this article by Matthieu Mandard. It distinguishes four key motives of referencing: epistemic, rhetoric, symbolic, and economic.

- Mandard, M (2021). **On the shoulders of giants? Motives to cite in management research**. *European Management Review*, DOI: abs/10.1111/emre.12495

In this classification, epistemic citations indicate the contribution of past authors, whereas rhetoric citations are mainly used to convince readers. In contrast, symbolic citations produce a representation of the researcher by drawing on the properties of citations. This might involve references to key journals or authors that have a symbolic function in the field. Finally, economic citations are used to provide rewards to the researcher themselves or their counterparts, such as editors and reviewers.

Of course, 95% of your references are simply there to support your arguments on a sentence-by-sentence level. This is what Mandard calls epistemic and rhetorical referencing. In those instances, you only need to decide there is how many references is enough (see also my blogpost on this topic: *"How many references is enough?"*). However, you can also use references more strategically and that's what this chapter is about.

How to use references strategically?

There are three ways to use references strategically: to set the scene for your paper in its introduction, to reference *relevant* publications by the editor or reviewers, and finally to reference core theoretical and methodological publications to signal which conversations you are participating in. The latter is what Mandard calls symbolic and economic referencing.

Setting the scene

In the introduction make sure you cite a few key and recent publications in the journal you submit to. Mind you, I am not asking you to comply with the dodgy practices of less salubrious journals that ask you to cite papers that were published in the last two years to boost their journal impact factor. However, by submitting to a journal you indicate you want to be part of the *conversation*; citing other articles in the journal is a way to acknowledge your conversation partners.

But do this only if the references are intrinsically important, i.e., they have an epistemic/rhetorical value too. Editors are not stupid, they can spot easily whether you have just added references to their journal last minute, maybe after having had your paper rejected at your preferred journal. So:

- Don't just cite ANY paper in the journal, but...
- Don't NOT cite any paper in the journal

If you really can't find any relevant articles in the journal to cite, you might need to reconsider your target journal. In order to find relevant articles, simply do a pre-submission check with the free Publish or Perish software to find relevant articles. Here is an example of how you can do this, it shows a search for articles published on language in the *Journal of World Business* since 2010.

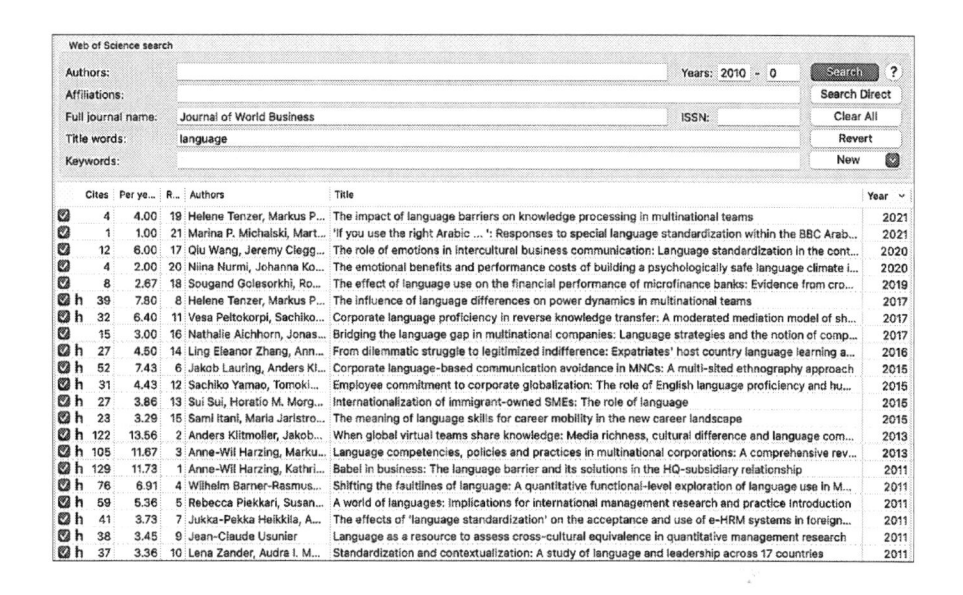

Reference the editor and/or reviewers

Second, make sure you reference key publications by the editor and likely reviewers (see also Chapter 12 dealing with writing a letter to the editor). This is what Mandard calls economic referencing. Again, I am not suggesting you do this to "flatter" or "bribe" the editor or reviewers, your references still need to have an epistemic or rhetorical value too.

However, try to put yourself in their shoes. Imagine that you have written a seminal piece of work on a particular topic. You are asked to be acting editor or reviewer for an article in which the author hasn't acknowledged any of this work. You are not going to be pleased, are you?

So, look up the editor and likely reviewers with Publish or Perish and read up on their relevant work if you haven't cited it yet. However, don't just "slip in" some references to people you think might be your reviewers by adding them to a block of other references. Make sure they are clearly relevant. (For detail, see my blogpost: *"Are referencing errors undermining our scholarship and credibility?"*).

Reference core theoretical and methodological publications

This is what Mandard calls symbolic referencing. Used like this, your references are "signposts", signals that you are part of the same conversation. They are shortcuts that can save you hundreds of words.

In your literature review, make sure you reference core theoretical publications (e.g., Bourdieu for social capital or Tajfel & Turner for social identity theory). In your methods section use those references that align with your research philosophy. Remember, every research method has its own core authors. This is even true for specific method *within* a particular research method.

For instance, in the broad field of Management there are three very different approaches towards analysing qualitative data: First, Kathy Eisenhardt's comparative case study method. Second, Denny Gioia's grounded-theory-based interpretive research method. Third, Anne Langley's focus on process research methods. By citing the "right" authors in your paper you can provide a clear signal to the editor, reviewers, and readers what they can expect.

Twelve guidelines for academic referencing

On a more general note, it is important to take referencing seriously. A lack of attention to accurate referencing undermines our collective scholarship. My first-ever published article, that written in disbelief during my PhD studies, showed how a range of referencing errors led academics to create a persistent myth of high expatriate failure. This myth was created by massive (mis)citations of three articles.

- Harzing, A.W. (1995) **The persistent myth of high expatriate failure rates**, *International Journal of Human Resource Management*, 6: 457-475.

The paper didn't quite have the impact I had hoped. Academics simply kept making the same (unjustified) assertions. A few years later, I therefore updated my analysis by including a much larger number of articles. More importantly, I also generalised my analysis to provide 12 guidelines for good academic referencing, discussed in detail below. I am pleased to say that this article now features on many PhD courses.

- Harzing, A.W. (2002) **Are our referencing errors undermining our scholarship and credibility?** The case of expatriate failure rates, *Journal of Organizational Behavior*, 23(1): 127-148.

1. Reproduce the correct reference

Include the correct information for bibliographic details such as the name of the author, the title of the article, the year published etc. There are too many articles that include small or even large errors in their references.

2. Refer to the correct publication

Many authors have published multiple articles on a topic. If that's the case, make sure you reference the *correct* article and don't just cite one of them "from memory". Don't assume that if you ensure you are representing the author's opinion correctly, it doesn't matter which article this appeared in. It does! So, just take the effort to find the correct article.

3. Do not use "empty" references

"Empty" references are references that do not contain any original evidence for the phenomenon under investigation, but refer only to other studies to substantiate their claims.

Subsequently, other authors then use these "empty" references to substantiate their claims rather than going back to cite the original source. This way, "empty" references can go through several generations with each subsequent author citing "empty" references that in turn cite other "empty" references.

In doing so, "empty" references create the appearance of a vast body of work supporting a particular claim, whereas in fact the "house of cards" is built on a – possibly very shaky – foundation of only one or two journals.

4. Use reliable sources

We expect academic articles to use *reliable* sources to substantiate their claims. That means that when for instance specific figures are quoted and references are used to support these figures, we would expect these references to contain solid *empirical* evidence for the quoted figures.

This is generally only the case in academic journals. So, treat data that either appeared in textbooks or in professional journals with caution. We can hope these sources conform to academic standards in terms of substantiating their claims, but, unfortunately, we cannot expect them to.

5. Use generalisable sources for generalised statements

When references are used to support a generalised statement (such as the fact that expatriate failure rates are high), we would expect these publications to contain evidence that is, at least to *some* extent, generalisable to the entire population (of expatriate managers).

6. Do not misrepresent the content of the reference

One of the most damaging violations of good academic referencing is misrepresenting the content of the referred article. In my case study of expatriate failure rates, there were quite a few references to articles that contained failure rates different from the ones they were purported to support, or did not actually contain *any* failures rates at all.

7. Make clear which statement references support

Many authors include a whole string of references behind a sentence or a paragraph that includes several claims. It is then not clear *which* reference is supposed to support *which* statement. So, ensure that your reference appears directly after the claim it supports.

8. Do not copy someone else's references

When you are doing a literature review, it is often tempting to copy references from another article on the same topic without checking the original sources. By doing so, however, potential referencing mistakes made by one author are given more and more credence through continuous reproduction by other authors. This is exactly how myths like the high expatriate failure rate myth are created and perpetuated.

9. Do not cite out-of-date references

When references are used to substantiate a particular claim that is either explicitly or implicitly stated to be valid at the present time, we would expect these references to be relatively recent. Many of the phenomena we are studying are subject to continuous change.

In relation to my case study of expatriate failure rates, even if these were high in the past, I would expect them to be lower now, due to, for instance, the increasing importance of global business, the higher levels of international experience, and companies' greater awareness of the need for cross-cultural training.

10. Do not be impressed by top journals

Or rather: be impressed, but do not be *so* impressed as to think that everything that appears in a top academic journal must necessarily be 100% true. Yes, it is true that standards at top journals are very high. However, their quality standards do not necessarily extend to verifying the accuracy of every single reference used in the article!

11. Do not try to reconcile conflicting evidence

Articles on a topic might provide conflicting evidence. Unless you are very familiar with the subject matter and the articles in question, it is best to report this conflicting evidence directly rather than to try to reconcile it. Reconciling conflicting evidence might easily result in distortion of the original claims.

12. Actively search for counterevidence

When presenting a literature review, it is the author's job to present *all* the relevant research. This means that it is the author's job not only to look for evidence that *confirms* his or her position, but also to look for and report counterevidence.

How many references is enough?

Like most senior academics I am reviewing a lot of papers, both for journals where I am on the editorial board and for my colleagues in the context of my staff development work at Middlesex. Many of these papers have sentences followed (or interrupted in the middle) by a long and sometimes **very long** string of references. Most of these papers had well over 100 references in total. So, I started wondering: How many references is enough?

More isn't always better

My "rule of thumb" has always been to use a maximum of three references to support a particular statement. The role of a literature review is to provide a **targeted** review of the literature. There are several reasons why it is wise not to use too many references:

1. It really disturbs the flow of the paper.
2. It may provide an implicit signal that your work isn't very interesting or important, as so much has already been published in the field. This means you need to work harder to convince the reviewers you are making a unique contribution.
3. It shows that you may not be able to distinguish what the key works in a particular field are and thus are not really that well versed in the literature.
4. It does make you look like a bit of a student as having lots of references is quite typical of PhD theses. So, it might lead the reviewer to think you are an immature academic writer, which is something you would want to avoid.
5. The more references you use (beyond the ones that are really needed to substantiate your argument), the higher the risk that one of the reviewers knows the work you cite better than you do and disagrees with you that this work supports the statement(s) you are making. This might lead the reviewers to be more critical of the rest of the paper as well.

The other side of the coin

On the other hand, there are also good reasons to not be stingy with references.

1. You need to demonstrate your thorough knowledge of the field by citing enough of the key references. If the field has been very active, this might mean referencing quite a lot of studies.
2. You need to cite the "key people" in a particular field for both intrinsic (it is what is expected in a literature review) and extrinsic reasons (they might be your reviewers and might be annoyed if you have missed their work). However, unless they are intrinsically important, don't "slip in" some references to people you think might be your reviewers by adding them to a block of other references.
3. You need to show you are part of the journal "conversation" (see also Chapter 5). Again, do this only when the references are intrinsically important. Editors are not stupid, they can spot easily that you have just added references to their journal last minute after having been rejected at your preferred journal.

General recommendations

As always, looking at your target journal will give you a better feel of the preferences in your sub-discipline. When doing a final read of the paper, you might also want to reconsider deleting references that you are only citing once and only in connection with a lot of others. These are clearly not essential to your paper.

Chapter 12:
Writing a letter to the editor

You are finally done with your paper. You have polished your title, abstract, introduction, and conclusion. You have even remembered to critically assess the references you are using.

So, now you are ready to submit to your target journal. After all this work you might be quite impatient to get your paper into the review process as quickly as possible. You might therefore be tempted to just skip the steps that allow you to provide reviewer suggestions and a letter to the editor. Don't! Doing so robs you of an important opportunity to shape the review process in your favour.

Picking your acting editor and suggesting reviewers

Some journals – especially those with a broad scope and many submissions – ask you to pick your acting editor from a list of associate and consulting editors. In most cases the choice is obvious as their different editors have a different disciplinary focus or expertise in specific research methods. However, if the list of editors features more than one associate editor in your research area, make sure to research their work carefully before making your choice. Using the free Publish or Perish software that you can download from my website will allow you to do this very quickly.

Many journals ask you for reviewer suggestions. I have heard some authors say: "*I can't be bothered to do any of this; I am not going to do the editor's job!*" I think that is both arrogant and naive. It is arrogant because it seems to suggest that the editor "owes" you something. An editor is an academic just like you, but one that is much busier, and also one who is sacrificing their own research time to take on an important academic service role.

It is also naive, because you are basically saying: I am not willing to assist you by providing a few suggestions that will help me getting the best possible reviewers for my paper. The editor might well think you don't care about how your paper is treated and be more inclined to suggest a desk-reject.

So please take reviewer suggestions seriously; usually the editor will take up at least one of your suggestions. And even if they don't, the list of names will be a clear signal about the specific conversation your paper is hoping to contribute to. I suggest you suggest at least 3 to 4 reviewers, but ideally offer 5 to 6 as many of those contacted to review might decline.

Normally, you would pick at least half of the reviewer suggestions from the editorial board. Again, make sure you perform a careful check of their publication profile before making your final choice. Have they published in this field recently (not 10-20 years ago), are they familiar with the research method you are using, are they likely to understand the country or industry context you are focusing on? Again, you can do this very quickly by using the Publish or Perish software. See also my blogpost: *"Meeting an official guest or your academic hero?"*

Remember that in most of the Social Sciences and Humanities, as well as some other disciplines, reviewers are not supposed to know who the authors are. The review needs to be "double-blind", i.e., you don't know who the reviewers are, and the reviewers don't know who you are. You should therefore nominate people who work in the field, but have not seen the paper before.

Obviously, you don't nominate people who you think would not like what you have done ☺. But it is a "no-no" to nominate people who know the paper, even more so if they are your friends or colleagues. They would have a clear conflict of interest that they would need to report to the editor. Needless to say, this is unlikely to improve the editor's disposition towards your paper.

What's included in a letter to the editor?

Most journals now allow you to write a letter to the editor. In the past, many authors simply skipped this step or included one or two polite, but empty, sentences.

These days, with the number of desk-rejects increasing, the letter to the editor has become much more important in many disciplines. It shapes the editor's impression of your paper. So, what do you need to include in such a letter?

- An explanation of why you have submitted your manuscript to that particular journal and why it is worth the editor's time to consider it. This could be good topics to include:
    - Why would your paper be of interest to the readers of that journal? How does it contribute to the conversation?
    - What are the key strengths of your paper? What are its main contributions?
    - Why is your chosen research site, industry, country, population, or method particularly interesting or relevant to the paper's topic?
- A list indicating who might be an appropriate acting editor and good reviewers for the paper with a brief explanation of why they are suitable.

In short, see the letter to the editor as your paper's business card. It should provide all the details the editor needs to get to know your paper.

How does this work in practice?

To give you an idea of how this would work in practice, I include some screenshots of a letter to the editor that we used in the paper on inpatriation that we discussed in Chapter 9: Introduction.

Why is our paper suitable for this journal?

First, we explained why we felt the paper was particularly suitable for *Journal of International Business Studies*.

> Dear Editor,
>
> Please kindly find attached our paper entitled: How does successive inpatriation contribute to subsidiary capability building and subsidiary evolution? A longitudinal perspective on inpatriates' knowledge transfer. We are submitting this qualitative case study to JIBS as we believe it extends and bridges the journal's recent conversations, especially regarding IHRM and global strategy.

What are our paper's key contributions?

Second, we outlined the paper's key contributions in some detail. Reading this again, I must admit I find it a little hard to "parse". So, I would recommend using shorter texts and bullet points to make it quicker and less burdensome to read for the editor.

> Our study investigates how inpatriation contributes to intra-MNC knowledge transfer and, in turn, subsidiary performance. Based on a total of 40 interviews and three forms of time-stamped archival data from Japanese MNCs, we propose a novel theoretical model. The model demonstrates the longitudinal process through which inpatriates' knowledge transfer contributes to building subsidiary capability and driving subsidiary evolution. As such, we bridge the IHRM and global strategy literatures by explaining how inpatriates' knowledge transfer provides strategic value to subsidiaries. In addition, our rich data provide qualitative insights into the micro foundations of individual knowledge transfer in MNCs. Specifically, we demonstrate how the individual knowledge that inpatriates acquired at HQ is converted into organizational knowledge upon their return to their original subsidiaries.
>
> Although recent research in IHRM has highlighted the diversified nature of global staffing practice and the value of inpatriates as knowledge agents, we still know little about the consequences of Inpatriates' knowledge transfer. Specifically, when compared to expatriation, the performance-related outcomes of inpatriation are largely unknown. Our study suggests successive inpatriation as a practical and effective process of intra-MNC knowledge transfer, through which a subsidiary can build its capabilities and evolve its role in the differentiated MNC network. Our findings suggest that inpatriation is not merely a staffing method that is complementary or secondary to expatriation, but a key practice in its own right to support subsidiaries' growth and development.

Acting editor and reviewers

Finally, we provided some suggestions for an appropriate acting editor and reviewers.

> Finally, we would like to recommend a suitable Area Editor and Reviewers for your consideration.
> - Area Editor: Dana Minbaeva. Among all JIBS Editors, her research expertise is most relevant to our paper.
> - Reviewers: Helen De Cieri, Mila Lazarova, Miriam Moeller, Torben Pedersen, Pawan Budhwar, and Paula Caligiuri. They are all important authors in research in the area of either IHRM or knowledge transfer, or both. Outside the JIBS editorial board David Collings, Florence Duvivier, Fabian Froese, and Arup Varma would also be suitable reviewers. In the interest of transparency, please note that some of these academics have co-authored a paper with the 2nd or 3rd author. However, to the best of our knowledge they are not aware of this manuscript.
>
> We acknowledge the very helpful comments from Helene Tenzer on earlier versions of our manuscript.
>
> Thank you for your time and consideration. We look forward to receiving developmental feedback from JIBS reviewers.
>
> Yours sincerely,
> Heejin Kim, Sebastian Reiche, Anne-Wil Harzing

Chapter 13: What else can you do to improve your chances?

You've polished your title, abstract, introduction, and conclusion to perfection, have critically assessed the references you are using, and have written a beautiful letter to the editor.

Is there anything else you can do to improve the chance that your paper is accepted? Yes, there is, although many of the things I am suggesting here are probably things you should have done earlier in the writing process.

First, polish the rest of your paper to perfection too, second get your name and work known as someone who knows what they are talking about, and third get advice from other academics and take an R&R seriously.

Polish your paper to perfection

Nothing puts off an editor or a reviewer like a big typo in the abstract or a forgotten word that makes the meaning of some of the sentences ambiguous. They might well interpret this as a lack of care, which can create a negative impression about the paper itself.

However, it is not just about typos. Every paper can benefit from a language edit. Very few of us are "natural" writers. An editor improves your English and clarifies your writing. This is true even for native English speakers!

If you are a non-native English speaker language editing is essential. English might be a relatively simple language to speak, but it is a very difficult language to write correctly.

Here are some common problems that I have encountered when reading my non-native English-speaking colleagues' work. These problems all occurred because of "language transfer", the application of linguistic features from one language to another. The more dissimilar our native languages are from English, the higher the likelihood that language transfer is problematic.

- Many languages do not have articles, or when they do, they do not differentiate between definite and indefinite articles; the distinction between these is crucial in academic writing (East Asian, Finnish, Russian).

- Some languages have fewer tenses than English; again, the distinction between tenses is crucial in academic writing (East Asian).

- The word order in a sentence in English is different from that in many other languages (incl. similar ones such as German and Dutch).

- Punctuation can change the meaning of a sentence completely in English. Many Germanic authors put commas in the wrong place.

- English vocabulary has more, and more subtle, nuances than many other languages; there are sometimes a dozen words meaning almost, but not quite, the same. Practice using the thesaurus to find the word that best captures your meaning.

- Some words in English might have two virtually opposite meanings, depending on the context (e.g., sanction).

Cannot afford an editor or proof-reader?

Here are some quick tips that might help you improve your paper.

- **Read the paper aloud sentence by sentence**. You will notice that by speaking the sentences rather than reading them, so can assess more easily whether a sentence "flows" naturally.

- **Translate the paper into another language, sentence by sentence**. When you translate a sentence, you often notice that the meaning of the original sentence is unclear or open to multiple interpretations.

- **Get someone else to read your paper**. When reading our own papers, we read what we think *should* be on paper, because we have the whole paper in our minds. When someone else reads your paper, they will only see what *is* on paper. So, they are more likely to spot errors and inconsistencies. You do not need to be an expert in the subject to read someone else's paper. In fact, it is better if you are not, though it does help if you are in the same broad disciplinary area such as the Social Sciences or Engineering. If the paper can be easily understood by someone outside your own narrow sub-discipline, it is more likely to be understood by the reviewers too.

- **Become someone else**. If you cannot find someone else to read your paper, become someone else. Let the paper lie for at least a few days, but ideally a few weeks. You will be amazed at how much you can pick up by reading your paper with a "fresh pair of eyes".

Get your name or work known

Second, get your name or work known. This isn't going to get a bad paper accepted. However, it may provide the extra 10% needed to change what is essentially a binary decision from "no" (i.e., a desk-reject or a rejection after review) to "yes" (i.e., put the paper into the review process or give an R&R).

This is probably more important at the R&R (revise & resubmit) phase than at the desk-reject phase. The R&R phase means that hen the editor has received 2-4 reviews and needs to decide whether to reject the paper or whether to give the author a chance to revise & resubmit it. As reviews are rarely unanimously positive, an editor is more likely to give you the "benefit of the doubt" if they know you as someone who is a competent author.

I am not suggesting that if you are a famous academic it is easy to get your papers accepted. Every academic, even if they are editors themselves or they are Nobel prize winners, gets rejections. However, if a journal editor knows you, has seen you present competently and with passion at conferences, or has read your work in other outlets, they are more likely to have the confidence that you will be able to revise the paper successfully.

Why is academic networking crucial?

If you are anything like me, your initial association with the word networking will be negative. When I grew up in the Netherlands it was almost a "dirty" word, and it seems I am not the only one who has this association. It implied that you got to where you were only because of your contacts, not because of any inherent skills, education, or good performance. This certainly was a big part of my initial reluctance to engage in academic networking.

However, after a while I to realised that academia is no different from "real life" in this respect. Just like "normal people" academics prefer to work with people they know and trust. Just like "normal consumers" they will also pay more attention to products (read publications) or recommendations (read references) from brands (read journals and universities) and people (read other academics) they know and trust.

Most academics have a very pressured existence. Moreover, both the number of academics active on a global scale and the volume of publications is rising ever more rapidly. This means you need to find a way to stand out in that stream of "clutter". Yes, most academics still do appreciate and recognise substance over packaging, but why not make it easier for them to find and appreciate that substance?

There are two key ways to get your name or work known. First to network at conferences and second to use social media strategically.

What is that conference networking thing about?

Despite the advent of social media, the best networking is still done face-to-face. So, whenever you have a chance, go to conferences, and *talk* to people. Rest assured: you don't have to be an extreme extrovert. I am certainly not, quite the reverse in fact. Don't forget that most academics are introverts, they are just *playing extrovert* for the duration of the conference.

But make sure you prepare. Decide who you want to meet before the conference, look up their background, and ask for introductions if necessary. Remember, most people like to talk about themselves. So, it is really all about asking the right questions. Be careful though: don't ask the world's most famous expert on a particular topic: what's your research about?

If you are not sure whether you are supposed to know your counterpart is a famous academic in your field, you can always ask "*what are you **currently** working on*" (with the emphasis on currently) or keep the discussion neutral by talking about the conference itself. If you are lucky, they reveal enough information for you to remember why you needed to remember them. If not, go to a quiet corner or the toilet as soon as you have a chance and quickly look the person up (assuming they are wearing their name tag). You then have another chance if you bump into to them again.

And don't worry, most famous academics are very nice people. So, even if you do blunder, they will generally forgive you. It might even make it easier for them to remember you. I once threw an entire cup of coffee over an important editor's nice shoes, but he is still speaking to me ☺.

Have your research brief ready

At the conference make sure you have your research brief ready. This is a short summary of your current research interests. Do create a few different versions, so that you don't just stand there "with your mouth full of teeth" as they say in Dutch (this roughly translates in English as: "be tongue-tied"), whilst mumbling something incoherent. Aim to have at least three versions:

- the 10-second elevator sound bite; it has to be short as you don't want to be half-way when you reach the right floor.

- the 1-minute coffee line version for when you are waiting in the same queue at the coffee shop; depending on the length of the queue, this can be expanded to the reception version.

- the 2–3-minute reception version, only use this when someone appears really interested; versions longer than this are probably best suited for sit-down dinners with like-minded academics.

Creating your research brief is hard. You might feel you are reducing your complex and varied research interests to a soundbite. But remember, the aim is not to be comprehensive, it is all about connecting with what you think the other person might find interesting.

So, what do I say? Well, it depends on what I think the background of the other person is, but it might be something like:

- One of my recent interests is the role of ethnic identity in the relationship between expatriates and local employees, when for instance ethnic Chinese Americans are expatriated to China.

- In my latest paper, I try to provide a new understanding of why Asian management practices are poorly understood by Western researchers.

- Lots of things really, but these days I am most interested in transferring my knowledge and experience about life in academia to young academics by blogging.

Social media networking

Obviously, you don't have to meet face-to-face to network. If you are unable to travel for family, health, or financial reasons, do consider using social media more actively. Using social media for research purposes is a big and multifaceted topic. I will be writing a separate book on this. However, below I have briefly outlined the key platforms that I think are most useful for academics.

Google Scholar Profiles

The one thing that every academic, no matter how time-poor, should do is to create a Google Scholar Profile. It is not strictly speaking a social media platform as there is limited scope for interaction beyond following an academic's updates. But it is an essential online CV, covering all your publications and their citations.

There is really *no excuse* for not doing this, setting up a basic Google Scholar Profile should not take more than 5-10 minutes. Not having a Google Scholar Profile might be quite problematic for an academic, especially if you are on the job market. I have heard a Dean say: s/he doesn't have a Google Scholar Profile so s/he can't be a serious academic.

For more detailed information about Google Scholar Profiles and their advanced options see my blogpost: *"Google Scholar Citation Profiles: the good, the bad, and the better."*

LinkedIn Profile

LinkedIn is very useful to present your basic CV online and connect with academics and non-academics alike. However, it can also be used to share news and to promote your own work. The advantage of LinkedIn is that it allows longer posts than for instance Twitter. It also usually has a more academic audience as most of your connections are likely to be fellow academics. Here are some suggestions of what you can do:

- Share interesting journal articles, newspaper articles, blogposts or any other material that has a LinkedIn share button and that is related to your (research) interests. I also share my own blogposts on LinkedIn and usually get a good readership, generally between 1,000 and 5,000 views.

- Write a short post on LinkedIn, for instance to alert followers to a recent publication or an event you or your university are organizing. You can find this option at the top of your timeline. If you can't find your timeline, click "Home".

- For something a bit more permanent, consider writing your own LinkedIn article. This is similar to a blog post and is a good alternative to blogging on a dedicated blogging platform. The advantage of doing this on LinkedIn you have a ready-made audience.

ResearchGate

ResearchGate is an online platform that allows you to create a list your publications (with full text where possible) and define research projects. It has become the "go to" place to find full-text versions of your papers, especially in the Social Sciences. Humanities scholars often use Academia.edu, a similar service, whereas academics in the (Life) Sciences and Engineering often use repositories such as arXiv.org. Increasingly though, academics from all disciplines are starting to use ResearchGate.

Unless you have a website of your own where you can upload full-text pre-publication version of your papers, ResearchGate is thus the "go to" place to offer full-text versions of your papers, something which is crucial to disseminating your work more widely. Even though I have full-text versions of all my papers on my own website, I still upload them on ResearchGate as well. I know this is where most academics are looking for them.

Blogging

When blogging started, it mainly featured online journals or diaries. These days it is simply seen as a way of sharing information with other people. For academics, this means sharing your research-based expertise. There are two main ways to engage in blogging: guest blogging on existing blogs or creating your very own blog.

If you want to try out whether blogging is for you, try guest blogging on an established blog. This doesn't commit you to writing more than one post and gets you a ready-made audience. There are a wide range of options: your own university's blogging platform, other universities' platforms, writing articles on LinkedIn, generic academic blogs, or even generic blogs such as Medium.

If you have acquired a taste for blogging, consider setting up your own blog. This provides you with the largest amount of flexibility to manage your own content. For my blog, I am using a content management system that has been custom designed for me and which integrates with the rest of my website. There are, however, plenty of free solutions – such as Blogger and WordPress – that allow you to start blogging straight away.

Twitter

Twitter is a micro-blogging site. Initially, I did consider Twitter to be utterly stupid and only useful for celebrities and people who were concerned with each other's breakfasts. However, I have found it a useful means to keep up to date with academic news. I have picked a lot of useful information through it that would have taken far more time to discover without using Twitter.

You can also share your own (and your colleagues') work and achievements. Tweeting about my academic articles, white papers and blog posts typically increases their readership five or ten-fold, sometimes *much* more. Not bad for a 280-character post! An unexpected benefit can be internal marketing, my Dean, Deputy VC, and VC all follow me ☺.

Get a "friendly reviewer" and take R&Rs seriously

Before submitting to a journal try to get a "friendly reviewer" who reads your paper critically. A friendly reviewer is someone giving the same kind of feedback that reviewers do, but is "on your side". However, you will need good networks to find someone willing to do this as you are asking them for a *big* favour. So, that's yet another reason to take networking seriously. And remember, you also need to be willing to "return the favour".

Once you are lucky enough to get a revise & resubmit, put yourself in the shoes of the reviewers *every single time*. Don't try to "set them right". Yes, I know that some comments might not be 100% correct, but neither is your paper. Remember these reviewers are your *peers*, that's why it is called peer review! Reviewers are not some almighty beings with full and perfect knowledge of any topic they are asked to review on.

Nor do they have unlimited time. Remember that these reviewers are sacrificing *their* scarce research time to provide their feedback on *your* paper. So, be respectful and provide them with a comprehensive and polite response. If you think some comments are incorrect or inappropriate, politely explain why rather than embarrassing them by demonstrating how stupid their comment is. Also consider that if they don't understand something, it might simply mean that you need to write more clearly or mention it at a different place in the manuscript.

Finally, if you do get your paper through the review process, make sure you celebrate properly before moving on to the next paper. In many disciplines, academics only publish 1 or 2 papers a year, if that. So, savour the moment, and do take some time to communicate the paper's message to a broader audience. That, however, is the topic of another book in this series, one that deals with the use of social media in academia.

Conclusion

This book was made up of two key parts. The first part discussed getting started with paper writing. It included chapters on the four Ps of publishing (Chapter 1), How to keep up to date with the literature (Chapter 2), Doing a literature review with the free Publish or Perish software (Chapter 3), Finding out which journals publish on your topic (Chapter 4), and Targeting the right journal (Chapter 5).

The second part of the book provided a structured 7-step approach to ensuring your paper gets past the first hurdle in the peer review process, the desk-reject phase (Chapter 6). It looked systematically at Titles (Chapter 7), Abstracts (Chapter 8), Introductions (Chapter 9), Conclusions (Chapter 10), Using references strategically (Chapter 11), Writing a letter to the Editor (Chapter 12), and other things you should do to improve your chances of acceptance (Chapter 13).

Having made it through these seven steps you should be ready to submit and have a good chance to at least get through the desk-reject phase. So, all that's left is keeping your fingers and toes crossed. If you should get a desk-reject after all, please do remember that the fourth P of publishing is Persist!

I hope this short guide has helped to demystify the topic of journal publishing and has provided you with the tools to be successful in your own publishing efforts. I would love to hear from you if you feel this book has helped you; feel free to get in touch with me at anne@harzing.com.

Further reading

My blog contains many more posts related to academic publishing, as well as academic careers more generally. Below I reproduce a partial list, structured by topic. Just Google the title and you will find them easily.

Publishing

The four P's of getting published
08 Dec 2016 – Anne-Wil Harzing
Short summary of my white paper explaining how performance, practice, participation, and persistence are needed in publishing academic papers

The four ailments of academic writing and how to cure them
20 Apr 2020 – Nico Pizzolato
Some golden tips on how to improve your academic writing

How to keep up-to-date with the literature, but avoid information overload?
14 May 2018 – Anne-Wil Harzing
Provides tips on how to keep up-to-date without getting lost

How many references is enough?
30 May 2020 – Anne-Wil Harzing
Some reflections on why more references isn't always better, but how strategic referencing might help

CYGNA: Writing a literature review paper: whether, what, and when?
19 Sep 2021 – Anne-Wil Harzing
Reports on our 41st CYGNA meeting on the challenge of publishing literature review papers

Want to publish a literature review? Think of it as an empirical paper
23 Apr 2021 – Tatiana Andreeva
What to consider if you want to publish a literature review paper

How to avoid a desk-reject in seven steps [1/8]
10 May 2020 – Anne-Wil Harzing
Introduces a 7-step process to increase your chances of getting your paper into the review process

Who do you want to talk to? Targeting journals [2/8]
24 May 2020 – Anne-Wil Harzing
Explains why choosing your target journal is the most important step in the publication process

Your title: the public face of your paper [3/8]
14 Jun 2020 – Anne-Wil Harzing
Illustrates how to create a good title through an iterative process

Writing your abstract: not a last-minute activity [4/8]
28 Jun 2020 – Anne-Wil Harzing
Explains what needs to be included in an effective abstract

Your introduction: first impressions count! [5/8]
11 Sep 2020 – Anne-Wil Harzing
What are the elements of an effective introduction: context, importance, and interest

Conclusions: last impressions count too! [6/8]
18 Sep 2020 – Anne-Wil Harzing
Why conclusions are a crucial part of your paper's key message

What do you cite? Using references strategically [7/8]
03 Oct 2020 – Anne-Wil Harzing
Shows you how references can save you hundreds of words and position your paper

Why do I need to write a letter to the editor? [8/8]
16 Oct 2020 – Anne-Wil Harzing
The last step in the submission process is an important means to "sell" your paper to the journal

From little seed to fully-grown tree: a paper development journey
09 May 2022 – Heejin Kim
A novice publisher providing a "behind the scenes" look at co-authoring for top journals

CYGNA: The wonderful world of book publishing
12 Dec 2020 – Anne-Wil Harzing
Reports on our 35th CYGNA meeting with three publishers discussing textbooks, research books and practice books

Own your place in the world by writing a book
11 Dec 2018 – Nico Pizzolato
A passionate plea to consider publishing a book at least once in your academic career

IB Frontline interview: mentoring section
03 Jan 2022 – Anne-Wil Harzing
Introduces the third section of my IB Frontline interview talking about my role as a mentor and my top tips for early career researchers

Career progression

CYGNA: Internal versus External promotion
11 Oct 2018 – Anne-Wil Harzing
Reports on our 22nd CYGNA meeting with a presentation giving tips for internal and external promotion applications

CYGNA: climbing up the academic career ladder
03 May 2021 – Anne-Wil Harzing
Reports on our 39th CYGNA meeting with a focus on career progression

CYGNA: How do I keep my job (in academia) in uncertain times?
13 Nov 2020 – Anne-Wil Harzing
Reports on our 34th CYGNA meeting discussing jobs losses in higher education in COVID-19 times

CYGNA: One size doesn't fit all – Diversity of academic career paths
28 Feb 2022 – Anne-Wil Harzing
Reports on our 45th CYGNA meeting in which we discussed four alternative career paths in academia

Open Syllabus Explorer: evidencing research-based teaching?
15 Nov 2019 – Anne-Wil Harzing
Reviews how the Open Syllabus Project can help academics to understand their impact on teaching and find the best textbook for their course

Presenting your case for tenure or promotion?
23 Nov 2016 – Anne-Wil Harzing
Shows how to make your case for tenure or promotion by comparing your record to a relevant peer group

How to create a sustainable academic career
21 Nov 2020 – Anne-Wil Harzing
Reports on Martyna Sliwa's presentation on career progression in the UK higher education environment

How to create a successful academic career: AIB – Ask, Invest & Believe
22 Jun 2019 – Anne-Wil Harzing
Write-up of my contribution to a conference panel on career strategies at the 2017 AIB-UKI meeting in Birmingham

CV of failures
15 Jun 2019 – Anne-Wil Harzing
Explains why rejection and failure are a normal part of an academic career and not something to hide or be embarrassed about

Publish or Perish increases transparency in academic appointments
14 Oct 2016 – Anne-Wil Harzing
Illustrates how PoP has been used to expose nepotism and incompetence

CYGNA: Careers, mobility and belonging: foreign women academics in the UK
02 Jun 2018 – Anne-Wil Harzing
Reports on our 15th CYGNA meeting with a special emphasis on the challenges for female foreign academics in the UK

Why are there so few female Economics professors?
11 Nov 2018 – Anne-Wil Harzing
Short summary of my article in Economisch Statistische Berichten on gender bias and meritocracy in academia

We need a different kind of superhero: improving gender diversity in academia
12 Jan 2021 – Jill A. Gould
Collects the resources developed for the 2020 AoM symposium on creating gender inclusive academic environments

WAIB Panel: Academic career strategies for women in the UK
01 May 2018 – Anne-Wil Harzing
Reports on a WAIB Panel at the AIB-UKI meeting in Birmingham April 2018

Research impact and funding

The four C's of getting cited
18 Sep 2017 – Anne-Wil Harzing
Short summary of white paper explaining why competence, collaboration, care, and communication help to realise the citation impact of your work

Everything you always wanted to know about impact...
02 Jun 2019 – Anne-Wil Harzing
Book chapter providing a quick overview of the what, why, how and where of research impact

Impact is impact is impact? Well, no...
20 Jun 2022 – Anne-Wil Harzing
Reprint of an invited blogpost on the SAGE Social Science Space on disambiguating the concept of impact

Research Academics as Change Makers – Opportunities and Barriers
13 Nov 2021 – Andrea Werner
Reports on a Middlesex University panel discussion on creating external research impact

How to make your case for impact?
13 Jul 2016 – Anne-Wil Harzing
Shows you how to make your case for impact by comparing your papers to the journal average

Making your case for impact if you have few citations
27 Nov 2017 – Anne-Wil Harzing
Provides advice on strategies to demonstrate impact with a very low citation level

How to ensure your paper achieves the impact it deserves?
15 Jan 2018 – Anne-Wil Harzing
Discusses the workflow I use to communicate about a new paper

How to find your next research project?
16 Jun 2016 – Anne-Wil Harzing
Provides suggestions on how to find new and interesting research projects

CYGNA: Working in a Horizon-2020 project
19 Feb 2021 – Anne-Wil Harzing
Reports on our 37th CYGNA meeting dealing with research funding and working in large, funded projects

How to write successful funding applications?
02 Nov 2016 – Anne-Wil Harzing
Provides ten tips for successful funding applications

Finding a Unicorn? Research funding in Business & Management research
05 May 2019 – Anne-Wil Harzing
Explains why university administrators need to be realistic in the amount of research funding they can expect Business School academics to generate

CYGNA: Positionality, team roles, and academic activism
27 Jun 2022 – Anne-Wil Harzing
Reports on our 47th CYGNA meeting, celebrating our 8-year anniversary with our first face-to-face meeting in 2.5 years

Social media

Social Media in Academia (1): Introduction
16 Jan 2020 – Anne-Wil Harzing
An introduction into my 8-part blogpost series on social media

Social Media in Academia (2): Comparing the options
28 Jan 2020 – Anne-Wil Harzing
General recommendations on how to use social media professionally

Social Media in Academia (3): Google Scholar Profiles
10 Feb 2020 – Anne-Wil Harzing
Provides recommendations on how to get the best out of Google Scholar Profiles

Social Media in Academia (4): LinkedIn
27 Feb 2020 – Anne-Wil Harzing
Provides recommendations on how to get the best out of LinkedIn

Social media in Academia (5): ResearchGate
09 Mar 2020 – Anne-Wil Harzing
Provides recommendations on how to get the most out of ResearchGate

Social Media in Academia (6): Twitter
27 Mar 2020 – Anne-Wil Harzing
Provides recommendations on how to get the best out of Twitter

Social media in Academia (7): Blogging
13 Apr 2020 – Anne-Wil Harzing
Provides recommendations on how to start with blogging

Social Media in Academia (8): Putting it all together
27 Apr 2020 – Anne-Wil Harzing
Final posting in the social media series explains how different social media can reinforce each other

Social Media in Academia: Using LinkedIn to promote your research
08 Apr 2021 – Christa Sathish
Tips and tricks for using LinkedIn to promote your research

How to digitally market yourself: a beginner's guide for students and academics
06 Nov 2021 – Christa Sathish
Handy tips and tricks to start building a digital presence

Other academic skills

Be proactive, resilient & realistic!
07 Jan 2020 – Anne-Wil Harzing
Argues that as an academic you are an independent professional shaping your own career

How to prevent burn-out? About staying sane in academia
12 May 2016 – Anne-Wil Harzing
Provides twelve suggestions on how to prevent burn-out and keep your sanity

CYGNA: Work intensification, well-being and career advancement
08 Dec 2019 – Anne-Wil Harzing
Reports on our 29th CYGNA meeting dealing with workloads and work intensification

On academic life: collaborations and active engagement
19 Jun 2018 – Anne-Wil Harzing
Discusses Martyna Sliwa's articles on the different rationalities underlying research collaborations and the need to get involved in managing and shaping the university organisations we work for

Want to impress at an academic job interview?
24 Jan 2017 – Anne-Wil Harzing
Shows you how to use PoP do some intelligence gathering to make a good impression at a job interview

CYGNA: Working effectively with support staff in academia
06 Mar 2018 – Anne-Wil Harzing
Reports on our 18th CYGNA meeting with a presentation on working with support staff and a discussion of boundaryless careers

CYGNA: Life-long learning in academia
03 Apr 2019 – Anne-Wil Harzing
Reports on our 25th CYGNA meeting with presentations on an Erasmus visit and participation in the Aurora program

How to hold on to your sanity in academia
11 Apr 2019 – Steffi Siegert
Steffi Siegert's powerful contribution that sums up everything that women can be facing in academia

CYGNA: Negotiation workshop
15 Feb 2020 – Anne-Wil Harzing
Reports on our 30th CYGNA meeting dealing with negotiation styles

How to promote your research achievements without being obnoxious?
01 Dec 2018 – Anne-Wil Harzing
Provides some quick and easy to implement tips on how to promote your academic work

CYGNA: Resistance to gender equality in academia
15 Mar 2021 – Anne-Wil Harzing
Reports on our 38th CYGNA meeting dealing with one of the ultimate gender topics

What is that conference networking thing all about?
01 Nov 2017 – Anne-Wil Harzing
Reflections on the importance of networking in academia and tips on how to do it

CYGNA: Supervising and being supervised
02 May 2022 – Anne-Wil Harzing
Reports on our 46th CYGNA meeting where we discussed our experiences of PhD supervision, both from a student and from a supervisor perspective

Meeting an official guest or your academic hero?
15 Sep 2016 – Anne-Wil Harzing
Shows you how to prepare for any academic meeting in 5-10 minutes

Printed by Amazon Italia Logistica S.r.l.
Torrazza Piemonte (TO), Italy